What Do T~~hey Say~~
When You Leave the Room?

How to Increase Your Personal Effectiveness
for Success at Work, at Home, and In Your Life

Brigid McGrath Massie, M.S.W., M.B.A.

with

John Waters

Eudemonia Publications®
P. O. Box 373
Salinas, CA 93902
(831) 757-8514

Index by AMC Indexing, Hollister, California
(408) 637-7567

Published in the United States by Eudemonia Publications, P. O. Box 373, Salinas, California 93902.

IBSN 0-9629850-0-7

DEDICATION

This book is dedicated to my life partner, Dan. Without his unfailing support, encouragement and faith it would never have been possible.

TABLE OF CONTENTS

1

INTRODUCTION:
A FLY'S EYE VIEW

Have you ever wished you could transform yourself into a fly on the wall? I have. It's a feeling that comes over me every time I blow a sale, fight with my husband or deliver a speech that leaves my audience yawning. The minute I leave the room I begin to wonder what I did wrong and what people are saying about me and my performance. And I long for the ability to buzz back, unseen, for a fly's eye view of their reactions.

Imagine what you could learn if you *could* become a fly on the wall. Forget the politics and soap opera stuff for a moment and just imagine what you could find out about yourself and your own personal effectiveness. Imagine the strategies you could develop, the improvements you could make, the shortcuts you could take.

This book was written to help you develop those strategies, make those improvements and take those shortcuts. It's not exactly a fly on the wall, but it will give you the information you need to become more personally effective. (And it's a lot cheaper than electronic surveillance.)

Now you may already be pretty darned effective. You may be an excellent engineer, ambulance driver, portrait painter, et cetera. You may be very good at your job. Well, that's great! And that's important, both to your bank account and your self esteem.

But, as important as it is to effectively execute the mechanics of your profession, it's really only part of the picture. Whether you're the very best butcher, baker or floppy disk maker around, I believe your success in your private and professional life ultimately depends on something else: Your PERSONAL EFFECTIVENESS.

WHAT IS PERSONAL EFFECTIVENESS?

Personal effectiveness is the power to direct your life. Sounds downright dangerous, doesn't it? Like a force only destiny should wield. But the truth is, we all have this power. We all "direct" our lives, whether or not we ever think about it in just that way. We all make choices, take actions -- or decide to do nothing at all. Then why, I hear you asking, do some people seem to have so much more of this power than the rest of us? Are they more talented? More intelligent? Are they psychic? Blessed? Genetically superior? Then they must have some special inside information, right? Bingo! Personally effective people aren't smarter or more gifted than their less effective peers. They just have more knowledge -- and a rock-solid determination to apply that knowledge to help them achieve their goals.

Unfortunately, an astonishing number of people just don't believe this. For more than ten years I've been designing and delivering customized training courses for large and small companies around the country. And in my work I encounter a truly amazing parade of otherwise perfectly intelligent people who believe that

2

personal effectiveness is an inherent trait, like blue eyes or red hair.

"Brigid," they tell me, "you're just naturally good at this stuff."

Don't I wish! But the truth is, I work hard at my own personal effectiveness. I take the knowledge and strategies I've learned and developed over the years and I apply them to my life every day.

Even more amazing to me are those people who believe personal effectiveness is somehow the exclusive province of the highly educated. Talk about putting the cart before the horse! I have a Master's degree in Business Administration *and* a Master's degree in Social Work, but I wouldn't have gotten either degree without first developing a high level of personal effectiveness.

Personal effectiveness isn't something mysterious. It's common sense, mostly. It's applying clear-cut strategies for coping with stress, managing our time and developing potent relationships. It's going after the recognition we need and deserve for our efforts. And it's developing our capacity for leading others.

As I've said, this book was written to help you with all of those things. It contains information and strategies culled from reams of clinical studies, stacks of self-help books and years of personal experience.

The quiz in the next chapter should give you a good idea of where you stand, personal effectiveness-wise. Take the quiz before you go on to the rest of the book, even if you plan to read it all. Your results will direct you to the chapter most relevant to your personal effectiveness problems. Then, take the quiz again in, say, six months, and then again in a year as a way of keeping track of your improved effectiveness.

Though each chapter can stand on its own, the material is arranged so that the preceding chapters support those that follow. All of the anecdotes are based on my experiences with the problems of real people. And all of the strategies *work!*

A fly told me so.

2

DETERMINING YOUR PERSONAL EFFECTIVENESS QUOTIENT

Just as the longest journey begins with just a single step, you'll want to track the growth of your personal effectiveness as you read this book. I've developed what I call the P.E.Q. or Personal Effectiveness Quiz to help bring to your conscious mind some of the attitudes and belief systems that might be hampering your personal growth. I'm not talking about religious beliefs here, though I acknowledge that they are important and a great source of hope and inspiration.

I'm talking about those subconscious beliefs such as, "I'm too old to be promoted." "Everybody likes me just the way I am." "I'm not smart enough to finish college."

These statements effectively prevent us from even *exploring* potential changes!

The first step is to flush these attitudes and beliefs out in the open where they can be exposed as obsolete, untrue or negative. Then you can apply the information contained in this book to change your behavior, which will change your attitude -- which I guarantee will change your life.

Don't struggle over your answers, usually your first shot is either right -- or you really don't know!

Just check "T" for true or "F" for false.

1. A personally effective person is always concerned about being promoted.
    T__   F__

2. Choosing friends based on their ability to help your career is an effective thing to do.
    T__   F__

3. Criticism is really valuable information.
    T__   F__

4. It is possible to maintain an effective personal relationship between a supervisor and a subordinate.   T__   F__

5. To be an effective leader, it is more important to listen, than it is to talk and direct.   T__   F__

6. People learn twice as much from your example as they do from your advice.
    T__   F__

7. To manage your time well, you have to eliminate most fun activities.   T__   F__

8. To be a true professional, you must be a college graduate.   T__   F__

9. Sharing highly personal information at work is OK if you are really upset.
    T__   F__

10. A "good" leader administers consequences -- both positive and negative.   T__   F__

11. Gossiping (the spreading of personal information that is almost always negative) is expected if you are going to be popular at work.   T__   F__

12. If you enter competitions for awards or promotions, you will be labeled as an egomaniac.   T__   F__

13. If your level of personal awareness is not expanding, you might have "plateaued."   T__   F__
14. Controlling your moods is essential to personal effectiveness.   T__   F__
15. Seeking professional help means you are not effective.   T__   F__
16. Most of the feedback that personally effective people get is negative. T__   F__
17. Even in a highly structured work environment, it is possible to create your own behavior.   T__   F__
18. Given an impossible situation at work or home, your alternatives are: change, accept, or leave.   T__   F__
19. Personal effectiveness is guaranteed by the time you are 40.   T__   F__
20. Most people are aware of what is said about them when they leave the room.
                                                  T__   F__

ANSWERS

1. FALSE. The goal of reaching higher personal effectiveness is *not* to be promoted, but it does happen more often to personally effective people. Promotions aside, having a high degree of personal effectiveness allows an individual to enjoy the intrinsic value and joy of work itself. One of my favorite quotes about my job is, "Doing what I love, and loving what I'm doing." See Chapter Five for more promotion hints and strategies.

2. TRUE. Choosing friends based on their ability to help your career doesn't mean tolerating

those with whom you have nothing in common, or those whose values clash with yours. Conversely, avoiding people whose influence, experience and contacts can provide strategic opportunities for you is senseless. The fact is, to maintain and promote your personal confidence you must affiliate with those you admire and want to emulate. The goal of effective and satisfying relationships is to become, "the person I always wanted to be when I grew up!" The information about relationships is in Chapter Seven.

3.   TRUE.   Criticism, when it is done right (which unfortunately it seldom is), can be solid gold. As is explained in detail in Chapter Three, you're vastly more likely to be criticized than praised. If you can cut through the personal innuendo -- grasp any helpful hints or insights -- those formerly hurtful comments can translate into an effective action plan for greater personal effectiveness. The trick is to gain enough confidence and personal insight to make criticism work *for* you, whether you are giving it or getting it.

4.   TRUE.   The Superior to Subordinate relationship is a very tricky one, so a careful reading of Chapter Seven is in order. Remember that "anything you say can, and will be used against you." Since supervisors play a powerful role in the awarding or withholding of job challenges and options, managing this key relationship can greatly influence your success and happiness at work.

5.   TRUE.   Listening has been called the forgotten art. Too often, "leaders" feel they must

have all the answers and solutions. Throughout the book, there will be references to "the workforce of the 90s," a group which requires new leadership and management skills. Chapter Ten addresses how you can mold *your* leading to *their* following -- for greater productivity and to increase your own personal effectiveness.

6. TRUE. In my opinion, the hallmark of a personally effective person is the congruency between their actions and their advice. Many of the examples in the book highlight people who are ineffective due to their "Do what I say, not what I do" behavior. Our peers, superiors and subordinates are not blind, and they judge us more by our actions than our words. See Chapter Ten for examples of "matching" your behavior to the situation effectively.

7. FALSE. Personally effective people are fun! They have learned key time management principles which allow them to have guilt-free play time. In fact, the thrust of Chapter Nine is to help you put more time *into* your life! If you have eliminated fun from your schedule, you probably aren't as personally effective as you could be. Read this important chapter for 15 ways to put more time into your life.

8. FALSE. Professionalism for a personally effective person is, "Someone who knows his/her job, and takes it seriously." This definition applies to plumbers as well as doctors. Chapter Six explores how to get help when you need it, freeing you to give your work the attention it deserves.

9. FALSE. Sharing personal information can destroy your credibility, impair your productivity, and it can even be used against you! Learn constructive ways to handle your stress, before it overflows and damages some of your key relationships at work. See Chapter Eight for stress management tools you can put to work at home and at work.

10. TRUE. Effective leaders administer *consequences*. Whenever possible, the consequences are positive. However, the quality of their leadership is often judged by their responsible attention to "what's broken." Problems that are ignored don't go away -- they grow! Effective leaders realize that performance has to be *managed*. Read Chapter Three to learn how to praise and criticize effectively.

11. FALSE. My theory is that "gossiping can be fatal to your career." Personally effective people not only refrain from exchanging highly personal information about others, they also prevent others from spreading it. Chapter Seven shows you how gossiping can harm both your career and credibility, and how to break this negative habit.

12. TRUE. Winning recognition for your work or volunteer efforts is crucial for three reasons. First, it gives you the pride and confidence to keep going and growing. Second, awards make you "stand out" so that opportunities and challenges are offered to you. Third, when the inevitable "down" times come, prior recognition can be a valuable tool for positioning yourself in an increasingly competitive environment. So, go for

the glory! Chapter Five explains that personally effective people realize that although other people might resent their accomplishments -- the intrinsic motivation of awards for their achievements is worth it. The Chapter also describes how to survive colleagues' jealousy, and how to enjoy your well deserved honors.

13.   TRUE.   Life is passing many people by. People do not realize that their hairstyle hasn't changed since high school or that they are "average Americans" who spend 6.5 hours per night hypnotized by television. Chapters Four and Six provide up-to-date, useful advice on "waking up and smelling the coffee."

14.   TRUE.   Mood control, the ability to control and isolate your emotions -- at will -- is a crucial skill for personal effectiveness. You don't have to adopt a "poker face" to be personally effective, but you must learn and practice being "situational." Being situational means that you can read clues from the environment and adapt your behavior accordingly. Chapter Eight, which deals with stress management, can help you to control your reaction to stressful situations.

15.   FALSE.   Using professional services can equip you for a quantum leap in your effort to increase your personal effectiveness. Chapter Six helps you to identify, use and benefit from the plethora of services designed to make your life easier, and you more personally effective. Just as our bodies catch colds, it is not uncommon for our minds to experience temporary (we hope), dysfunctional periods. With professional help you

can increase your personal effectiveness exponentially.

16. TRUE. Criticism, fair or not -- deserved or not, is a fact of life. Actually, most of the feedback that *everybody* gets is negative. By reading Chapter Three, personally effective people are able to "translate" criticism into personal and professional improvement.

17. TRUE. You can create your own behavior, regardless of your work environment. Chapter Four shows you how to create behavior that increases your effectiveness and maximizes your impact.

18. TRUE. Personally effective people not only realize they have choices, they acknowledge that they *deserve* them! If you feel your life or career has become a dead end, the insights into stress management in Chapter Eight should free you to begin to exercise some of your options.

19. FALSE. Age is not a guarantee of personal effectiveness. Just as some people "don't let college get in the way of their education." Working at becoming more personally effective, and creating an environment where *others* can experience success is a lifetime endeavor. Chapter Five shows you how to create success patterns in your life.

20. FALSE. Most people spend a lifetime worrying about what is said about them when they leave the room -- but until now they have been empty-handed when looking for specific ways to

make the changes they sense are needed. Others have told me they are overwhelmed with the awareness of all the changes they need to make, but don't know where to start. May I humbly suggest, with this book? *What Do They Say When You Leave the Room* represents solid, concrete strategies based on hundreds of interviews, conversations and seminars I have given to people just like you who are ready, open and determined to grow!

DETERMINING YOUR PERSONAL EFFECTIVENESS QUOTIENT

To determine your present level of personal effectiveness, tally your "score" and consult the ranges that follow. Remember, in a quiz like this, finding out what you got right is not as important as finding out what you don't know. This book is designed to help you increase your personal effectiveness as expeditiously as possible. Therefore, you can go directly to the chapter indicated if there is a specific area you are concerned about, or simply read straight through the book to get a "big picture" perspective.

15 to 20 correct
You have demonstrated a high degree of personal effectiveness. Still, this book can help you gain new insights and strategies to keep growing.

9 to 14 correct
Like most people, your "education" has not included coaching on some of the new areas of personal effectiveness training. What sets this book apart from other "self help" books is the practicality of its suggestions. Read on!

0 to 8 correct

Your willingness to open this book indicates a timely commitment to change. Read and reread the suggestions -- try one change at a time -- and, congratulations on your decision to grow!

3

NO PAIN, NO GAIN:
GIVING AND GETTING
CONSTRUCTIVE FEEDBACK

"I'm only telling you this for your own good!"

"If only someone would tell him about how his use of the term 'girls' alienates him from his own sales force!"

It often seems as though most of the feedback we get in our day-to-day lives -- even in the most loving and supportive of environments -- is negative:

"You're too fat."

"You're late again!"

"You could do better if you tried."

Many people I've worked with confess that they see the sources of feedback in their lives as downright dangerous, like little defective microwave ovens regularly bathing them in invisible, noxious radiation. Yet, just as all radiation isn't harmful, all feedback isn't negative. In truth, we all need lots of feedback in our lives to be truly effective, and most of us need to learn to generate more of it!

I can best illustrate my definition of "feedback" with a simple formula:

Feedback = praise + criticism.

Unfortunately, the words "praise" and "criticism" are charged with meaning for most people. They imply -- and rightly so -- that someone is making a judgment. But that's what feedback really boils down to: judgment.

Fortunately, my dictionary offers a definition for "judgment" that is a little less incendiary than its usual connotation. According to the Oxford American Dictionary, feedback is the "...*return of part of the output of a system to its source...*" or "*...the return of information...*"

The return of information; I like that definition! Sometimes feedback is praise, and sometimes it's criticism, but it's always information -- information that is vital to your personal effectiveness. Thus the formula becomes:

Feedback = Information.

Why is this information so important? Because without it, your picture of your own personal effectiveness will be incomplete, like a half-drawn diagram of a house you'd like to renovate. You need a complete, accurate, warts-and-all blueprint of the structure you've got or the structure you set out to build will be misaligned and unstable. Your roof, as it were, will leak, and your personal effectiveness will collapse into a pile of sticks in the first stiff wind.

EXAMPLE. I recently consulted with a political campaign organization that was trying to improve its effectiveness. The group leader, Molly, was an intelligent, talented woman with an extremely strong personality; one of her campaign workers described her as an "all or nothing" type of leader. "The all," the worker told me, "is her. And the nothing is everybody else."

As I worked with the group, I soon learned that this particular worker's opinion was shared by nearly everyone on the campaign. And as I observed Molly's behavior, I began to agree with that opinion myself. I can sum up her leadership style this way: she treated people like BIC lighters; she fired them up until she burned them out and then she threw them away.

The problem with treating people like cheap disposables is that, after a while, they tire of it. Then they won't support or follow you any longer and your effectiveness as a leader evaporates. (See Chapter Ten: Leadership.)

After a while, it became clear that, for all her individual ability -- which was considerable -- Molly's personal style was diminishing her group's overall effectiveness. Non-verbally, she was getting tons of feedback from her workers in the form of crashing silences at meetings and unfriendly to outright insolent behavior. I eventually interviewed most of the workers in the group and asked them why they didn't just come out and tell her what effect her behavior was having on them.

"Why bother," was the common answer. "She doesn't listen. She doesn't care."

And the sad truth was, Molly didn't care. When I discussed the issue with her, she insisted that I had interviewed chronic complainers who just couldn't cut the mustard. She never listened to their criticism, she said, and in fact, discouraged them from contributing at all. Why should she listen to them? No one knew more than she did about the campaign. She admitted that she was sometimes abrasive and even rude to her workers. But she believed that was what she had to do to get the job done.

17

Despite Molly's unwillingness to listen to any voice but her own, (certainly not, as she believed, because of it), the group won the campaign. But 80 percent of the people who worked to win that victory failed to show up at the victory party. Many of the workers I had interviewed swore later that they would never again work on a political campaign of any kind.

Molly was surprised and hurt by the scant turnout. But, true to form, she blamed the poor attendance on petty jealousies. She failed to see that her former workers were trying like hell to tell her something. She failed to recognize the value of a very important source of feedback.

Molly's failure was masked by her success and she soon found herself leading another group, this time a community fund-raiser. Though virtually none of the people she had worked with on the campaign signed up to work with her again, there were plenty of new eager feet waiting to fill their empty shoes.

And, with scarcely a pause for reflection, Molly proceeded to stomp those feet flat. As before, her workers resented her tactics. They clammed up, held back; communication ceased utterly. The group's effectiveness was, as before, diminished.

But unlike the smooth running political campaign, the community fund-raising campaign was fraught with problems. Unexpected problems. Problems Molly couldn't have anticipated. Problems Molly didn't even know existed because no one bothered to tell her about them.

And, of course, she never bothered to ask. Molly plunged blindly and deafly on, raising little money and making many enemies.

But let's not be too hard on Molly. Few of us willingly accept personal criticism; much of it really is negative and about as useful as smog. And for all her bluff and thunder, Molly was simply too insecure to see personal criticism as anything but threatening. But if she had listened carefully, she could have heard, amid the grumbling, the reasons her fund-raising efforts were not working. She could have seen that the fund-raising group was simply not as well prepared as the political group had been. Molly's considerable talents were desperately needed in unexpected areas. She could have made adjustments, sought help, and unleashed the competence of others, not to mention the fact that Molly could have collected a lot more money.

Learn from Molly and her mistakes. Think of the feedback in your life as a mirror provided by the people around you, including those people you are trying to work with, influence, or from whom you are trying to solicit love and support. A careful look at that mirror can reveal volumes about how you're doing. The cost of turning away from that mirror, as Molly found out, can be high.

MIRROR, MIRROR

The very best strategy I know for generating effective feedback from others is simply this: Learn to give it yourself. Once you learn to give it, you will be much better at recognizing the good stuff when it comes bouncing back to you. Remember: Feedback = Information.

Information pulled from effective praise and criticism, that is.

What exactly do I mean by praise and criticism? Glad you asked.

19

In my opinion, one of the most useful definitions of praise can be found in *Putting the One-Minute Manager to Work,* by Ken Blanchard and Robert Lord. To paraphrase: praise is the act of catching someone doing something right. It's taking the time to say, "Gee, Bob, great job on the Whizbang account! Getting that report in on time was very important to me. Way to go!" It's a positive way of articulating expectations and reinforcing the kind of behavior you like and want continued.

Praise is a reward.

Praise is a process that facilitates social relationships. Done well, praise creates trust and it bolsters the self-esteem of both the sender and the recipient of the praise. Praise is also a powerful tool for motivation. Why? Because we all seek attention. It's human nature. Praise is *positive* attention. When you praise people, you notice them at their best. We are so often noticed at our worst -- or ignored altogether. Receiving praise reinforces your own self-esteem and solidifies your positive image of yourself from the person offering the praise.

Many people feel that if praise is a reward, criticism must be a punishment. But I disagree. Criticism is not the opposite of praise. Both are processes, ways of imparting information. And, done well, criticism produces the same result as praise.

My dictionary defines criticism as: "...*the act of making judgments, finding fault, censuring, disapproval...*" Unfortunately, people spend a lot of time using this process in destructive ways.

A manager I worked with, for example, was well known in his company for his effective budgets. But he was equally well known for being unable to work well with his staff.

"There's no middle ground with this guy," a staff member told me. "He's a zero-to-sixty kind of manager. You're either gold, or you're dog meat."

This manager's only response to inappropriate or unwanted behavior among his staff members was "censure" -- which is certainly one form of criticism. But, not an effective one.

THE MANAGER AS PARENT TRAP

The reason many people fail to use praise and criticism constructively at work is that they simply don't know any better.

After all, the only experience many people have with praising and criticizing is as a parent or a child. And, of course, this type of relationship works well *only* in the context of the family. In business, you can't hug an employee or give him a cookie afterwards. Additionally, the more you assume a parental role with people, the more childlike the behavior you tend to elicit from them in return.

They Are Afraid to Rock The Boat

EXAMPLE. The publisher of a small business journal was quite good at most aspects of his business, but he had a tough time managing certain types of people -- namely, artists. One staff layout artist and graphic designer threw tantrums when anything she designed was criticized. "Whenever I say anything, she blows up," he told me. "She acts like a child! But I don't know what to do. If I say anything, I won't have an art department."

So, rather than lose her, the publisher let her get away with murder. She was an artist, after all, and they're, well, temperamental. Right?

Wrong. By letting this artist get away with her unprofessional behavior, the publisher engendered an incredible amount of resentment from the rest of his staff, all of whom were artists, too, by the way.

In the end, the publisher was forced to fire her or lose his whole art department.

You can avoid the publisher's dilemma by observing the following guidelines for effective praise and criticism.

Set Ground Rules

Ground rules are crucial to effective praise and criticism. You need job descriptions and established, agreed-upon procedures if you are ever going to have a standard with which to compare the performance of your workers.

In companies which choose to do without these standards, it's very tough to praise or criticize. But even more important, supervisors who fail to establish ground rules, sabotage their efforts to praise or criticize. However, if you say from the outset "I am responsible for your performance and your effectiveness in this job. You can trust me to tell you when you are doing well; you can trust me to tell you when changes need to be made," you have established that all important basis for praise and criticism.

Don't Wait For A Crisis

Some managers wait until the situation is so bad, the only alternative is firing. But by waiting for a crisis to develop, they in fact create one. They create the opportunity for more and more people to model the dysfunctional behavior of the very employee they refuse to criticize. And they miss many opportunities to reinforce effective behavior by failing to praise.

TWO SIDES OF THE SAME COIN

You might be surprised to learn that praise and criticism are remarkably similar processes, really two sides of the same coin. But knowing that, you shouldn't be too surprised to learn that many of the same rules for effective use apply to both.

Timing

For both praise and criticism, timing is absolutely crucial. The best time to praise an employee, for example, is when he's down -- not when he's just won the Salesman of the Year Award. Certainly you pat him on the back when he's doing a good job; he expects and deserves it. But he doesn't really *need* it. He's on top of the world. But when that same employee is down, he does need praise. And that's when praise is most effective.

EXAMPLE. Say you've just started a job as a receptionist. You're a good worker, but the phone system is new and you're nervous and you've missed three calls in a row and you've just cut off an important client. Now is when you need praise for the two calls you did take. Now -- right now -- you need some encouragement to motivate you to carry on and do your best and master the phone system. If your boss comes in and says, "Good grief, you missed all these calls? What's wrong with you?" chances are remarkably good that you are going to give up.

The time to offer criticism, however, is when the person you need to criticize is feeling good about himself. After the aforementioned secretary has gotten a handle on the phone system and the boss has noticed her accomplishment, she's much more likely to hear and respond to his criticism that her skirt may be inappropriately short.

RULE OF THUMB. How receptive people are to your criticism depends more on how you deliver it than how they receive it. So, if you wish to criticize, you must be in control of yourself. Your fists cannot be clenched. Your voice cannot be raised. You must communicate non-verbally that you are criticizing the person's *behavior*, not the person.

Privacy

In the military they say, "Praise in public; criticize in private."

I'm a Navy brat myself, so I say this with more than a little trepidation: Ahem... I disagree. (Sir!)

I strongly believe that both praise and criticism must be offered in private if it's to be effective.

(Note: A striking characteristic of the workforce of the 90s is that it absolutely thrives on praise. Standing up before a large group of these workers and saying, "You're all doing great!" is going to be about as effective as knitting with over-cooked spaghetti -- and just about as long-lasting. It's too diluted to be meaningful.)

Praising individuals in public doesn't work because it sets people up to be knocked down by the petty jealousies that are an inevitable component of every group. It implies that the other people present haven't been doing as good a job as the subject of your praise -- which certainly may be true. But just because it's true, doesn't mean you have to rub everybody's face in it; not if you want them to strive to improve their own performance.

If you want your praise to have a lasting effect, literally motivating your people for years, you have to pull those people aside individually and give it to them in private. The company may need a little public *Rah-Rah* now and then, but individuals need private, individual praise.

The same rule applies to criticism. It nearly never makes sense to humiliate people in public. They won't listen -- and they'll never trust you again, and neither will the other people present during your tirade. Even if you do your criticizing calmly, keeping the person's best interests at heart, you must do it behind closed doors if you want it to have a positive effect on that person's performance.

Don't Overdo It

Whether you are praising or criticizing, you've got to know when to shut up. Employers who over-praise, for example, run the risk of losing their credibility. Eventually their praise will be seen as insincere and manipulative.

Over-criticizing has a similar effect. While you are ranting and raving, your audience has stopped listening, and is thinking, "Geez! I may have been wrong, but it's not like I murdered anybody or sold military secrets to terrorists. I don't deserve all this!"

So keep it short. Plan what you say ahead of time. This way whatever you want to say, either

25

positive or negative, will be brief and to-the-point. And that's how it should be.

Judgment

Most of the people you praise or criticize are bound to believe that you are judging them. And, let's face it, folks, they're dead right.

There's no reason to flinch in the face of this interpretation. We all judge the actions of the people with whom we interact. Praising or criticizing is simply voicing those judgments.

If you are a manager, supervisor or some other kind of authority figure, judging is your job. Abdicating this responsibility can sap your effectiveness more quickly than any other move you can make. It can have very destructive consequences for everyone.

EXAMPLE. A teacher is supposed to judge his students' performance. But suppose your daughter's teacher decides, since the news is bad, to let her off the hook without appropriately criticizing her schoolwork, hoping that her next teacher will accept that responsibility. Before you know it, your daughter is graduating from high school and she can't read.

Be Specific

If you want your praise or criticism to be effective, you must be specific. This is absolutely essential, and it's harder than you might think. "Well, Suz, you're doing a great job," just won't cut it. Neither will, "You've got to straighten up your act, Bob." These comments are too general; they have no place in effective praise or criticism.

Comments like, "We all really appreciate what a hard worker you are, Susan," or, "You've just got to start acting like a team player, Bob," are also too generic. Neither of these statements is specific enough to be really effective. Susan may, in fact, be a hard worker and Bob may not be much of a team player, but telling them so won't get you anywhere because you've framed your praise and criticism *in personal terms.*

You must keep in mind that, to be effective, praise or criticism must be directed at a person's behavior. And that means you have to do some homework in advance.

EXAMPLE. Susan is a hard worker and you want her to know how you feel about it so she'll be inspired to keep it up. Ask yourself this question: What specific task has Susan accomplished? What was it about the way she handled it that was good? How was it important to me and the company (family, group, etc.)? Answer these questions and you are prepared for a quick, effective praising.

Or: Bob is operating a little too independently and not working well with the team. Ask yourself: What specific examples can I list which illustrate this behavior? What is the specific effect on the team and the team's goals? What should Bob be doing instead? After all, Bob isn't an unrepentant scum. He's just not working well with the team right now. His current behavior can be changed with the right criticism.

Why do you have to be so specific? Because if you're not, you can do more harm than good. Meandering praise will be viewed with suspicion, and general criticism will leave the recipient depressed and powerless. There's nothing to be gained by general personal attacks. Specific criticism of specific actions -- with specific solutions

-- will actually empower the recipient and, possibly inspire the kinds of changes you are looking for.

Watch Your Motive

The most important question you can ask yourself before you praise or criticize is: Why am I doing this?

People in general, and employees in particular, are suspicious of praise and criticism -- and with good reason. A quick look at the history of workplace racial, religious, sexual and age discrimination -- not to mention out-and-out harassment -- should give you a good idea why. "You're criticizing me because I'm black," or "You're praising me because you want to go to bed with me," are not far-fetched claims. And, unfortunately, the same situation often exists between family members and friends.

So, to effectively praise or criticize, you must recognize this and deal with it.

The best way to begin is to take some time to stop and think about your own motivations. Ask yourself why you are choosing to praise or criticize this person at this particular time. Are you angry? Are you trying to improve things, or are you just venting your frustration? Do you know specifically what you want to accomplish? And, most important, how is your goal in praising or criticizing this individual going to help him/her?

This last question is the most important. In order to effectively praise or criticize, you must want to help the person to whom this praise or criticism is directed. "I am not criticizing you so I can lay you off, Ed, I'm trying to make you more effective at your job so we can both stay employed."

Or: "I'm really not harping on this homework thing so you will be miserable and I can brag about your grades, Junior. I honestly want you to have the skills you need to make it in this world."

Or: "I wanted to let you know about what a good job you did because it's very important to the company that you keep up the good work -- so important that there's bound to be a raise in it for you."

If you can't praise or criticize with the other's best interests at heart, it's better for both of you to say nothing at all.

Pay Attention To The Feeling

The last similarity between praise and criticism can be found in the feelings each produces. That statement may seem a bit odd at first reading, but it's true.

Think about it. While getting bawled-out for chronic tardiness certainly won't make you feel as good as being handed an employee-of-the-month plaque, both feelings are going to stick with you for a *long, long* time.

These feelings are so powerful they can change people's lives. That's true of adults and children alike -- even seniors. In fact, it's while working with retired seniors that I've found the best examples of the incredible lifespan of these feelings. When I asked a retired mail carrier recently what he remembered most vividly about his job, he didn't mention any of the many raises he received during his 20 years with the U. S. Post Office. Nor did he speak of his retirement benefits. "What I remember when I think about my years on the route," he said, "is the day my boss said to me,

'George, you are the fastest mailman we ever had on this route.'"

Those words have echoed in George's mind for well over 40 years. He hears them today as clearly as if his boss had said them yesterday.

DOS AND DON'TS OF PRAISE

Powerful, darned-near everlasting emotional responses are created whenever you praise or criticize. In short, you're playing with dynamite, folks; you have to handle it with care.

Do Make It Meaningful

Whenever you praise, keep in mind that what you say or do must be meaningful to the people you are praising or it won't be effective. This will take a little detective work on your part. Some people respond best to a little *Post-It* note on their telephone. A smile works best for others. For some, a pat on the back works best.

Cautionary note: Appropriate touching by supervisors, teachers, *et al*, is, sadly, a big issue nowadays. So make sure that your pat lands in neutral territory; somewhere between the hand and the shoulder and definitely above the belt. And bear in mind, too, that for some people, there is no such thing as appropriate touching.

Do Make It Concrete

Whatever strategy you employ, make a conscious effort to document your praise, to write up something good as well as something bad. In some organizations, people have to wait a whole year before they are given some concrete evaluation of their own performance. What people want is a piece of paper that says, "You did something right."

What *you* want is to reinforce good performance. Documentation helps everybody win.

Do Use It Frequently
Reinforce that behavior! "Everybody's been on time all week. That's terrific! Look how much more we got done. Good for you!" Use praise. It works.

Don't Forget Top Performers
It's been observed that there is nothing more unfair than equal treatment of unequals. "Why should I knock myself out doing twice as much if nobody notices?" People know when they've done an outstanding job -- and if you want that kind of performance to continue you better notice it too!

Do Be Specific
It is incredibly important to give people specific praise for specific behavior. They want your praise, sure, but they also want to know what it is specifically that they did well. And they want to know how to do more of it so they can continue to receive praise.

Do Show Your Sincerity
It's absolutely critical to be sincere when you praise. If you're just gushing, your employees are going to know it. They'll think, "Oh, great! She's gone to another seminar on employee relations! I wonder how long this will last before she goes back to her old, nasty self."

Don't Overdo It
Adjust to circumstances. People who haven't praised very much tend to go overboard

with it. Think about what the person you want to praise has done. How important is it? Establish a scale in your mind. Don't damn them with faint praise, but don't sweeten them into hypoglycemia, either.

Do Ask for Input

A lot of employers, parents and others are actually afraid to ask the person they want to praise what sort of reward they would like. But it's one of the best ways I know to make your praise really effective. Oh, sure, an employee might say something like, "Well, Boss, $50,000 would go down mighty smooth right about now." But then he's going to laugh and shrug and ask for the afternoon off to go to his son's Little League practice. Or he'll mention that his chair is giving him a backache, or that he needs to make a dental appointment but he's been afraid to since the company has been so busy.

Don't assume that everybody wants a bonus or the day off. Ask. They'll kill for you if you do.

Do Incorporate Praising In Your Management Style

For some people, this will take time. Not everybody is a natural praiser. You are going to overdo it or underdo it or just plain blow it at first. But keep at it. Look for opportunities to make people feel better about their work (and, in the process, you too.) Then, someday, when you are arbitrary and unfair, or when the execs upstairs instruct you to do something rotten to those you supervise, you will find people more cooperative and more understanding. And you will be remembered for more than your lousy disposition.

Managers who praise properly, credibly and regularly, find their jobs are much easier. People trust them and are more comfortable interacting with them. Their relationships with those they manage improve because, hey, it isn't always bad news. That is a highly motivating person to work for!

And the best managers are the ones who work with and through other people effectively.

DOS AND DON'TS OF CRITICISM

Giving criticism is a little trickier than giving effective praise, but you must master the art of effective criticism to be truly personally effective. In many cases, folks, it's your job.

Do Criticize To Prevent A Mistake

Clearly, people do make mistakes at work. They make them because of lack of experience, lack of judgment or they may just not know how to do it right. We always look for good intentions, but sometimes they do it deliberately: Ralph sabotages Jennifer's project; Herb is drunk on the job.

Whatever the cause of mistakes, they must be addressed or they will continue.

Do Suggest Changes

Unless you are in the military, and in the position of issuing orders, you must frame your criticism in the form of a suggestion if you want anyone to listen to you. Always "suggest" to adults. Adults aren't children and you don't want them to act like children.

This is one of the most important reasons for criticizing in private: It allows the recipient the chance for rebuttal. Sometimes they have legitimate reasons for their behavior that you should know about. "I only made one sales call because I spent four hours showing the video." "Oh, man, you don't have to show the video every time!" "Nobody told me."

Remember, this is feedback you want. The last thing you want is someone who stands quietly by and says, "Okay, Boss. Anything you say." That person has just turned you off completely.

Don't Include Value Judgments

Remember that you are criticizing their behavior, not them, personally. "When you come in late it puts the whole office behind schedule," is different from, "I'm so disappointed in you. This shows how lazy you are." Adults are not going to listen to the latter comment, and if they're not listening, what's the point?

Do Criticize to Improve Performance

Most people do underrate their abilities and their productivity. Specific suggestions showing how people can improve their performance can be quite welcome in many circumstances.

Don't Lose Control

It still amazes me how often I hear stories about managers who get phone calls and then immediately charge out into the plant, screaming and yelling and looking for blood. If you are going to criticize effectively, you must stop and get control of yourself. And while you're at it, get the facts. Nothing will give your criticism as much credibility as sure knowledge.

Do Take Responsibility

One of the most common mistakes you can make when criticizing is trying to gather support for your position from others. I've seen supervisors head for the break room after criticizing an employee to talk with the other supervisors about it. "Yeah, I really raked Barnes over the coals this morning. But, hey, I had to, ya know?" They know all right, and that's just the problem. If you go into the break room or pick up the phone and talk things over like this with the other supervisors in your company, not only will other people in the company overhear you, but when the employee in question is transferred to a new supervisor, he goes with a tarnished reputation -- long after the original problem was solved.

And if you want your employees to change their behavior, if you want them to trust you and not start a word-of-mouth campaign against you which will severely impair your effectiveness, you've got to keep your mouth shut, too.

Also, stay away from comments like, "Hey, if it were up to me, I wouldn't say anything. But you know the boss." Or, "Look, it's not just me. I've talked to everybody in your department and they all agree." The first statement dilutes the effectiveness of your criticisms, without dulling the sting. The second statement exacerbates the employee's feelings of insecurity. *"Oh great,"* he thinks. *"Everybody in the joint is against me!"* Which of course, is destructive, de-motivating and not true.

Do Be Specific

Just as with praise, generalizations don't belong in effective criticism. Let people know *specifically* what they have done wrong, as well as what you want them to do next time.

Don't Try to Soften The Blow

Some managers think it's important to lighten things up with a little joking around before they drop the hammer. That's nonsense! These managers aren't putting anyone at ease and they aren't fooling anyone. Employees know when they are in trouble. By joking around, these managers are saying that they aren't important enough to merit seriousness. If it's a serious problem, be serious.

But also keep things in perspective. Some problems are certainly more serious than others. You don't want to be a "zero-to-sixty" type of manager; it's just not effective. All criticism should proceed from some sober, honest point. Be specific and constructive. Give suggestions for next time. And leave the joking for the office party.

Don't Compare

Never compare one employee to another. If you hit them with statements like, "You should be more like Sheila," they'll update you on the spot on all the dirt about Sheila. So now Sheila is in the discussion! You want to talk to and about only the person with whom you have a specific problem.

And besides, comparisons are by their very nature, unfair. Sheila can always be on time because she doesn't have three kids to get off to school and day care. The only comparison you should make is *an individual's performance to a job standard, description or generally accepted procedure.* Leave other people out of it.

36

Don't Over-Criticize

To those people who say one-on-one meetings with employees are too time consuming, I say, they won't be if you do it right. If you are clear about what you want, it should all be over in a few minutes. Once you see that they understand the problem and know what it is you want them to do about it, it's over.

Don't Say "Always" Or "Never"

This may seem like a small issue of semantics, but it's very important in maintaining your credibility. Statements like, "You're always late," or "You never wear a tie," leave no room for hope. It's not necessary or effective. Use phrases that acknowledge an alternative to behavior.

Don't Use The "Sandwich Technique"

I hear more arguments about this than just about anything else, especially from the military. The "sandwich technique," for those of you who haven't heard of it, goes like this: First you tell the employee something good about them, then you hit them with the criticism, then you end it with a, but-you're-okay-anyway, type of statement. It's the most predictable, Psych 101 approach there is. It doesn't work with adults. They know better.

Far from softening the blow, the sandwich technique makes people feel worse. When I talk to people who have been caught in the sandwich, they tell me they feel like they've been run over. "I'm good, but I'm bad, but I'm good," an employee of a large manufacturer told me shortly after her run-in with a sandwich-making manager. "He's full of it! Now I don't know where I stand!"

If you know specifically what you want an employee to change, there's no need to shy away from direct criticism. In fact, if you do it well, it will even sound like praise -- without the artificial masking the sandwich technique employs.

The truth is, employees become extremely motivated when they are properly criticized. They know what to do differently. They know where they stand. They know what the boss likes and what she hates. They know that if there's another problem, she will tell them; they won't have to wait a year to find out.

Effective criticism enhances job performance and satisfaction because, once employees know where they stand, they can concentrate on those areas the boss wants them to concentrate on. They can look forward to fewer screw-ups. If they thought four widgets per day was enough but the boss thinks it should be ten, they can now make a choice. "Am I going to make six more widgets a day or am I going to go somewhere else?" They no longer have to read your mind. They can relax and do their jobs.

PITFALLS AND PRATFALLS: WHEN PRAISE AND CRITICISM DON'T WORK

Praise and criticism, as I've already said *ad nauseum*, is a tricky business. Even the most experienced supervisor can easily take a false step and end up with his foot in his mouth. So, as you begin to give this kind of feedback, be on the lookout for the following eight most common pitfalls of praise and criticism.

Read My Mind

Does this sound familiar: "What are you talking about? We've worked together for years; this problem must be obvious to you, too!" Or how about this: "What is the matter with you? Do I have to spell it out for you every single day? Can't you see what I want here?"

The answer to that last question is, most likely, a resounding "No!" "But how can that be true when we've worked together for so long," you ask, "and the problem is so obvious?" It's true because no one can read your mind.

This statement seems so obvious to me that I almost left it out of this book. That would have been a perfect example of this very pitfall. You can't assume everybody knows what you know, thinks as you think, or does as you do.

Failure to put out praise or criticism in a concrete, constructive way can lead to tremendous polarization. Employees can "feel" they know what they are doing right, or "sense" what changes are needed -- but fail to make them because they are unclear on the proper direction. Don't turn your company's morale or your team spirit into a popularity contest. Spell out what you like and/or dislike, and keep the channels of communication open. In most of the situations I've encountered, both personally and professionally, in which people are polarized, it has been the result of this kind of assumption. Avoid this pitfall by beginning all your praise and criticism reading from the same sheet of music as those to whom you are speaking.

Last Quarter Amnesia

Unfortunately, because of the fast pace at which we live our lives, most of us remember only what happened yesterday. In other words, whether we mean to or not, we suffer from a faulty and selective memory.

So you have to ask yourself, "If all I can remember about this employee's performance is her work during the last few months, am I really clear about her overall effectiveness on the job?"

The answer to this question, of course, is "No." Maybe she was really cooking for the previous nine months and you've just lost it all in the fog of everything that's happened since.

Avoid this pitfall by keeping informal notes about employee performance throughout the year. That way, you will be able to better assess whether a particular employee's behavior reflects some sort of short term flare up, or reveals a long term trend.

Form Phobia

Before you sit down to write up a performance appraisal, take a minute to write one for yourself. It's one of the best ways I know to test the effectiveness of the form. Get familiar with the vocabulary so you are consistent. Make sure the words are, in fact, meaningful. If you're using the same performance appraisal form for the guy who types the letters as the one you use for the guy who loads the product onto the trucks, it's time to set up a new system.

The Statue Of Liberty Syndrome

Have you ever thought, or worse, said this: "Oh you poor, inadequate, undereducated (fill in the blank), I'm not going to expect anything from you so I probably won't get anything from you. But that's okay. We're working under difficult circumstances, so you can be a marginal performer."

You might as well add, "And so can I," to that sentence, because if you are falling into this trap, you are a marginal performer, indeed. *Send me your tired, your poor...* This may be okay for Mother Country; for you, it's a huge mistake! I often see this behavior in firms where the employees are encouraged to think of the company as a family. Don't kid yourself; if you cut people so much slack you never expect a darn thing from them, they are going to let you down. Then, not only will you be an ineffective supervisor, you'll be an unemployed one.

Appraisal Avalanche

Don't leave your appraisals for the last minute! They take time and they are crucially important! Appraising the performance of workers is one of the most important jobs a manager or supervisor performs. Be sure to schedule enough time to do the job right. And remember, a lot of turnover occurs at the same time, so many appraisals come due about the same time. Plan, and you won't be buried in paperwork.

Super Sally Syndrome

This is a tricky one (aren't they all), and it's very common. A Super Sally isn't necessarily super at all. But the manager, supervisor or parent who falls victim to this syndrome thinks he/she is super. In fact, in the eyes of the afflicted supervisor, Super Sally emits a kind of glow.

But that glow is only in the eyes of the beholder. You see, Super Sally Syndrome sufferers (say that three times fast) view certain people (usually those who reflect an earlier version of themselves) with a kind of tunnel vision. A super-aggressive sales manager is very impressed with a super-aggressive salesperson. An executive who is a single mom is very sympathetic to the receptionist who is recently divorced and is struggling to manage her job and her kids.

So what's wrong with this syndrome, you ask? Looks to you like a dandy opportunity for a little mentoring, you say? What's wrong with seeing yourself when you were a little farther down the ladder, you wonder?

What's wrong in this case is this: Your job, whether you are a supervisor or a parent, is to manage this person. If your vision is clouded by memories of yourself, you won't be offering the kind of feedback you need to be effective. Your own prejudices and biases will knock you both down before you know what hit you.

Told you it was tricky. If you find your vision is super-clouded, it often makes more sense to have the appraisal done by someone else.

NO PAIN, NO GAIN

Giving and getting feedback can be -- let's be honest -- a very painful experience. So who wants pain? Isn't it easier to just let people slide? I won't promote her. I won't use that vendor again. No raise for him. That sounds better, doesn't it?

Easier, maybe, but not better. An easy way to see just how destructive it is to avoid giving and getting feedback is to think of the old adage, "the chain is only as strong as its weakest link," or "one rotten apple spoils the barrel." You bet it does. Besides, it's your job to identify, confront and solve problems -- including people ones!

BE TRUE TO YOUR SCHOOL

Have you ever heard a statement like this: "Ernest, a lot of people have come to me over the last several weeks about you and we need to make this change. It's really not me, you know. I like you and I don't think there's a problem, but..." Or this one: "Look, Ralph, all our salespeople across the board are being zapped. The unfeeling creeps in New York have eliminated your job. It's not just you kid..."

Both of these statements are utter nonsense and the guys on the receiving end know it. Don't fool yourself into thinking that the praise and criticism you must dole out are not yours. If you do, you lose your credibility. And without that, your words mean nothing.

Make your praise and criticism effective by *owning what you are saying*. Stand up straight and say what you've got to say. Tell them that you've seen this and this, and this is how you feel, and this is what you want them to do about it, and leave it at that.

Nobody likes, trusts or believes a wimp.

4

IDENTIFYING WHAT WORKS...
AND DOING MORE OF IT!

Personally effective people create their own behavior.

Now I know that sounds like I'm declaring that sweaters knit themselves, but it's true.

Take some time to look around a little and you'll see that this is not such a startling statement after all. Pick the most personally effective person you know: the salesman who is always on time, even when traffic jams the freeway; the speaker who always pronounces everyone's name correctly, even the Japanese ones. Buttonhole that person for a minute and ask her how she manages to keep it together all the time.

I'll bet you the price of this book no one you ask answers, "Heck, it just comes naturally."

In my work as a professional speaker, I sometimes ask my audiences this question: "Do you think speakers use a script? Or do we just stand up here and speak from the heart?" A surprising number of people confess that they think I'm talking off the top of my head.

Well, I hate to spoil my image as the impromptu wizard of the lecturn, but I not only use a script, I practice like crazy. I study my topic and my audience. I create the behavior that will make my speeches (most of them) successful and my seminars effective.

None of the personally effective people I know -- and I know a lot of them -- would think of wandering out into the cold cruel world without a consciously refined Script for Success which I call Behavioral Standards.

Of course, we all have Behavioral Standards, even personally ineffective people. Of course, their Behavioral Standards hinder, rather than enhance their performance.

EXAMPLE. Ron is a salesman with a Midwestern grocery wholesale operation. He's smart and he's a hard worker, but it seems like he hasn't left the dock since he launched his sales career 12 years ago. He puts in the hours and he covers the territory but he doesn't make many sales for all this trouble. And the few accounts he does manage to land don't stay landed for long.

Driving to meet with a prospective client, Ron worries about his sales presentation. He's met with this prospect three times before and he knows he is not well liked because he was late all three times. He's not really as sure about the prices this time since there have been some changes lately and he hasn't had time to check them. There was really no time to check the presentation ahead of time, either, and the thing is not typed up right; it's full of typos and, oh man, the prospect's name is spelled wrong! And there's a spot on my tie! And...Jeez! Where is that calendar with my next appointment?

Obviously, Ron is heading for disaster -- not to mention a traffic accident if he doesn't stop looking for his calendar while he's driving. But his failure has been literally preordained by a set of Behavioral Standards of which he is probably not aware. These standards consistently steer him away from success.

Ron's Behavioral Standards are riddled with self-defeating behaviors. Self-defeating behaviors are those actions and words, gestures and habits that un-do all our efforts to be effective.

Some examples of self-defeating behaviors include;
* using profanity in a professional environment;
* an inability to sincerely compliment someone else;
* cooperating in a character assassination or standing by and letting one happen;
* not being able to accept a well-earned compliment.

If you find yourself often saying, "Oh no! I didn't do that again, did I?" you've got a problem with self-defeating behaviors.

In Ron's case, he has unconsciously told himself that it's okay to meet with his client late, unprepared and sloppy. It's okay to fill his head with visions of failure. It's okay to stumble along unconscious of his behavior, and its effect on others.

Well, none of it is okay if Ron wants to make a sale or keep a customer. However, once he becomes aware of them, he can choose to eliminate his self-defeating behaviors. He can choose to engage in the kind of behavior which will make him personally effective. In other words, *he can create his own behavior.*

In order for any of us to make this kind of change, we must first become conscious of the behavior we are currently choosing and how it either supports or sabotages our efforts to become personally effective.

EXAMPLE. Susan is anything but aware of the particularly destructive self-defeating habit she has developed which is sabotaging her career.

No one can say that Susan is not good at her job. She is consistent and efficient at most of what she does, and during the seven years she has worked as a teller at a Northern California bank, she has performed well, if not exceptionally well.

But every Monday morning, her supervisors and co-workers seem to avoid her. They go out of their way to avoid her, like boxers dancing away from left hooks. Why? Because those unlucky enough to find themselves cornered by Susan on a Monday get the full weekend load of bad news.

Susan is always the bearer of bad news, and it's always personal. Her daughter's teeth are bad, her husband has a drinking problem, her sister is having a nervous breakdown -- and of course, she overate all weekend. Sometimes it's the neighborhood, or the I.R.S.. Sometimes it's the job.

Though she doesn't notice, her co-workers feel embarrassed and burdened by these personal revelations. They sometimes offer helpful advice, which Susan never seems to take, or even listen to. So they feel foolish and avoid Susan, who grows more and more isolated, while remaining totally unaware of the damage.

Susan is disclosing personal information that others should not, and probably do not, want to know. Remember: Anything you say can and will be used against you! Without knowing it, Susan is committing character suicide.

By constantly talking about herself, Susan is also missing two very important opportunities for personal effectiveness:

1)   She is failing to learn about other people because she is not listening; and, more importantly,

2)   She is failing to learn about herself because she's not generating feedback.

If you follow the strategies outlined in the previous chapter, you will begin to actively generate and analyze feedback from your friends and associates -- even strangers. You will create a mirror in which you can view an accurate reflection of your current behavior, and the behavior you want to, or need to, change.

Now let me ask you a question: What do you see?

It seems like a simple enough question, now that the communication lines are open and the information is finally coming in. But to look at the mirror is one thing. To really see what's reflected there, some of us have to have it broken over our heads.

If your answer to the above question is, "I see an aging middle manager who's had some bad breaks," or "I see a novelist who's selling real estate," you are probably looking at your mirror with one eye closed and a rose colored monocle over the other one.   And if you say, "I see a hopeless failure!" or "I see an incompetent loser," both eyes are probably tearing up from the pain of your hair-shirt.

Of course, none of these statements are truly accurate.   They fog your reflection with either positive   or   negative   justifications   for   your behavior. They keep you from taking a clear and hard look at where you are now and what you did to get there. Without a judicious application of some psychic cleaner to your mirror, you cannot possibly make the kinds of choices that will make you personally effective.

In other words, personally effective people do not whine, justify, or apologize. They see clearly that they do what they do, whether they are receptionists or presidents of companies. They see that, in the immortal words of Popeye the Sailor, "I yam what I yam."

If you could read the mind of a personally effective person, you might hear a declaration like, "I'm all grown up and I really am a shoe salesman and I'm not gong to pretend I'm something else." That is a very effective -- and downright powerful -- statement, because the person making it is taking responsibility for his or her situation in life.

I'm certainly not saying that you have to remain a shoe salesman if you'd really rather be a teacher, a house painter, or a Rocky Mountain tour guide. Far from it! And I'm not saying you have to change your profession to become more personally effective. I'm saying that to be effective, you must own the decisions you have made and the situations those choices have created.

If it doesn't belong to you, you can't do anything to change it.

Owning who and what you are is the absolutely essential key to becoming personally effective. Once you begin to develop the habit of looking at yourself and your behavior clearly, you can begin to recognize the need to engage in behavior which is directed toward what you say you want from life. If you can do that, the rest will be a piece of cake.

PERSONAL EFFECTIVENESS EXERCISES

Here are two simple, but surprisingly effective exercises that will help you get a fix on where you are right now:

First, using 3 X 5 notecards, write the following:

"I'm all grown up now, and I really am a (blank), and I'm not going to pretend I'm something else."

Now fill in the blanks with your current job title: "I really am a plumber, receptionist, assistant manager, housewife."

Use the other cards for anything else you've learned about yourself through the feedback exercises: "I really am ten pounds overweight." "I am the life of the party." Or, "I'm always late." "I love to take care of young children and am recognized as an expert." "I'm intolerant of my co-workers." "I feel undereducated for the position I hold."

Some of the blanks will certainly be filled with things about yourself that you want to change, but you can also probably list a few things that you don't want to change. The idea is not to beat yourself up, but to recognize and accept who you really are right now.

And remember: this is an exercise to help you see where you are right now, not where you will be forever.

The second exercise is designed to help you become more sensitive to the feedback you give yourself: your self-talk.

51

You'll only need about 15 uninterrupted minutes -- and a timer, something with a bell or an alarm so you don't have to look at it to see when your time is up -- to complete this exercise. It's very important to be insulated from telephones, children and other distractions for the entire time.

First, sit down at an uncluttered desk or a table somewhere private and get out a pad of paper -- a legal pad works well -- and a pen or pencil that you particularly like to write with.

Now relax, sit comfortably, and set the timer for three minutes. As soon as the timer is set, quickly begin writing anything that comes into your mind. Anything. Don't take time to think about what you are writing, just write.

Write your grocery list. Complain. Swear. Be positive, negative, or both. Write "blah...blah...blah..." if you have to, but keep the pen moving. You are doing this exercise correctly when you manage to write continuously for the entire three minutes.

At the end of the three minutes, stop and take a look at what you've written. Don't worry if some pretty negative things appear on that yellow paper. (Researchers have found that for most people 70 percent of what they continuously repeat to themselves is negative.) No one will see what you have written but you -- just as no one hears your self-talk but you.

Look for apologies, excuses, and justifications for not changing. The first step in any action-oriented plan for improvement or change is awareness. You can't change what you do until you change what you say on your internal tape of your conscious and unconscious thoughts.

Having evaluated your self-talk, you're now ready to restructure and reshape that talk with the help of the information and exercises in Chapter Five.

Dealing with what people say when you leave the room starts with controlling what you say to yourself. You have taken an important first step to become more aware of, and in charge of your self-talk. You're ready now to flex your mental muscles and utilize your new awareness to influence how *others* view you.

5

THE SECRETS OF BEING SELECTED

If you were sitting on a shelf in a grocery store, would I buy you? Sounds like a silly question, I suppose. Few of us would willingly categorize ourselves alongside disposable diapers and bathroom grout. In fact, to anyone with a reasonably high level of self-esteem the question is probably rather insulting.

"I'm a person!" I hear you shout, indignation oozing from every self-assured pore, "Not a product!"

But the truth is, when it comes to personal effectiveness, that's exactly what we are: products. People in all areas of our lives, from bosses and clients to lovers and friends, "buy" us in myriad ways everyday -- and they're all smart shoppers, folks. Before they buy, they take a good look at our "labels," our "prices" and our "packages." They are drawn to us in the first place by our personal "advertising." To make sure we're selling what they're buying, we conduct ongoing "product research." And the time we have to make the sale is limited, because, like all perishable products, each of us has an "expiration date."

But before I send you off to the shrink-wrap machines, let me put this notion into a meaningful context. "Product" is, of course, just a word, and, in this case, a metaphor for each of us and what we have to offer others. "Buy" is also a metaphor, but a less offensive expression might be "select." Whichever word you prefer, I believe that thinking of ourselves as products is exceedingly useful for two reasons:

First, it accepts reality. Whether we like it or not -- plan for it or not -- people buy/select us each and every day of our lives. At work, our bosses literally buy our services, determining our value in monetary terms. At home, at church or in the community, others determine our value in intangible ways, selecting us by choosing to give us their love, friendship, affection or trust.

Second, this product metaphor provides us with a clear model of our personal effectiveness. It focuses our attention on the features and benefits we have to offer. It reveals how those features and benefits stack up against our competition. And it shows us what the "buyers" in our lives perceive those features and benefits to be worth.

Do I still hear some grumbling out there? Hrmph! Well, I was prepared for this. For the benefit of those squeamish readers unable to swallow the idea of being bought, we'll switch to the "select" euphemism. (No offense, folks. It works just as well.)

EIGHT SELECTION TIPS

Thinking of ourselves as products, far from diminishing us, allows us to apply proven marketing strategies that can make us significantly more effective. In other words: If it works for running shoes and breakfast cereal and cars and tissue paper and aspirin and microwave ovens and television sets and button-fly jeans and everything else we eat, wear, watch or drive, why can't it work for us?

The answer is: IT CAN. And the sooner we recognize our "productness," the sooner we can take steps to make sure everything about us, from our label to our price tag, supports our goals and aspirations.

#1.   *When It's You On The Label*

Ever attend a social gathering, say a community fund-raiser, where the minute you walk through the front door you're confronted by a garrison of elderly women stationed at two crepe paper covered card tables handing out name tags? Most of us have. Ever tried to escape without being tagged? It can't be done! These cadres of blue-haired volunteers are not chosen arbitrarily, folks. No, these are crack squads of labeling ladies who can slap a 3X5 sticky-back tag onto your lapel before you can smell the cheese dip.

But suppose for a moment, you stroll into one of these events and, instead of asking for your name, one of these Magic-Marker wielding mercenaries says this:

"Label please."

"Huh?" you quip.   "Label!" the volunteer replies, looking up from her 10-mile scroll of computer paper. "What's your label?"

Now what do you say? Does she want your job title? Your marital status? Your age? Height? Education? Astrological sign? Income?

"Gee, ma'am, I don't think all this is going to fit on a 3X5 name tag."

You bet it won't. Your "label" is much more than any of those things: it's the total effect of dozens of verbal and nonverbal messages we send to each other on both a conscious and unconscious level. It's your *image*. It does includes your name, job title and marital status, among other bits of information from your resume, but the truth is, most of us have made up our minds about each other long before we ever hear any of those details.

You see, we are, first and foremost, animals. We instinctively size each other up, employing all our senses. And we begin that sizing-up process immediately. Before language kicks in, we've sent and received dozens of sensory messages. In the first few seconds we've noticed such things as posture (slouchers seem weak; people who stand erect seem strong), personal odors (some people smell clean, positive, inviting; others have a body odor, cologne or perfume that is overpowering -- if you don't think this is important, ask the people who petitioned to have Giorgio perfume banned on elevators in L.A.), and the handshake (a firm, strong grip is appealing; a death grip, clammy hand or Princess Di finger grip is off-putting).

Once we begin to speak, what we say is not as important as how we say it. Our sense of hearing is either assaulted or engaged by the person's voice. The type and manner of greeting, syntax, vocabulary and grammar, and most important, volume, all have an effect (she mumbles like a shy teenager; he screams like a pro football coach; she speaks too slowly; he speaks too fast).

Then there's eye contact. I coach people not to use Superman eyes -- there's nothing to be gained from trying to stare people down with your X-ray vision. But staring down at your shoes won't work either. When we meet people who gaze at us calmly, keeping their eyes focused in a relaxed way somewhere between the top of our heads and our shoulders, we feel as though they are giving us their full attention and that we are being accepted. It creates a picture -- an *image* -- that's worth a thousand words.

Personally effective people are acutely aware of the effects of these fundamental messages. And they learn to control them -- and, thus, the images/labels they create -- by first determining what signals they are sending (see strategies for generating feedback in Chapter Three), and then determining what those signals mean to the receivers. Only then can they take the necessary steps to redesign their labels.

These steps don't have to be drastic. They might involve something as simple as putting on a suit and tie. That's the way one Rotary Club member I know manipulated his label to get himself elected club president.

EXAMPLE. Harold's label was "Retired Farmer" and he knew it. I know he knew it, because that's how he introduced himself to me when he first asked me to speak at a meeting of his club. He also confessed that, though it was a label he was proud of most of the time, resonating as it did with earthy sensibleness and honesty (qualities, I later discovered, he possessed in great amounts), it had several drawbacks.

"Let's face it," he said, "to most people, farmers are not considered particularly 'professional'. Oh, we're smart -- a lot smarter than most people think. And we're tough; just look at these hands. But professional? Someone who speaks well, is well informed and can lead a community service organization? *Naw...*"

Well, this farmer could do all of those things with one rough hand tied behind his back. Harold was a very capable man. He had proved it through a lifetime in a profession that required him to master several disciplines (agronomy, sales, marketing, management, animal husbandry and auto mechanics, to name a few). But he was a quiet fellow and, though he had aspirations for a leadership role, had always found himself drifting to the background.

Harold knew that his label was part of the problem. No one would believe that a sun-burned old geezer in overalls and a seed cap could serve as a proper representative of the Rotary Club. He recognized the way he was generally perceived and he took steps to change that perception.

As I said, it wasn't a big step. All Harold did was put on a conservative business suit -- he was already clean and friendly and articulate. It didn't happen overnight, but eventually, it transformed him, literally, from "redneck" farmer to Rotary Club president.

Not all labels are that easily sloughed off. Some people may have to do considerably more than change their clothes to create a new label for themselves.

EXAMPLE.   Lupe was a computer programmer who was having trouble finding a job after the company where she worked for nearly ten years suddenly went belly up. Her credentials were impeccable and she was invited to many interviews, but no offers were forthcoming. She called me one day for some advice. I found her to be pleasant and articulate and we arranged a meeting at a local restaurant. She told me to look for a woman with short, black hair.

But Lupe's dark hair wasn't her most striking feature. As she walked through the restaurant entrance, I spotted her job search problem instantly. Though she stood only about 5'4", she must have weighed at least 250 pounds!

We talked frankly for several hours about her job search. She was as quick and well-spoken in person as she was on the phone and I liked her. I told her that, while I was certain she would be an asset to any employer, I suspected she was the victim of a prejudice -- almost universal in this country -- against overweight people.

Lupe told me she hadn't always been heavy. In fact, when she first started working after college she was quite thin. But three children and a career of sitting before a CRT all day long had taken its toll and before she knew it she was casting one heck of a shadow.

So my comments came as no great surprise to Lupe ("You mean I'm *fat*? No kidding!"), but she hadn't really recognized how this affected her label; or what it meant to her job search. What it meant was, most people would never see that she was a competent, dependable, experienced programmer who worked hard at her job. What it meant was, the only thing most people would see when they looked at her was a "fat girl" (not even "fat woman," for crying out loud). And that is a powerful message, one which carries with it connotations of bumbling, Oliver Hardy/Lou Costello stupidity and overall undesirability that obliterates most other considerations.

What we are talking about here is *perception*. It doesn't count that Lupe was, in fact, quite good at the job she was applying for. The human animals who interviewed her couldn't get beyond the signals her physical appearance was sending them. Her "fat girl" label kept her unemployed.

Lupe had two options for dealing with her label, now that she understood its effect on her job search. She could go on a diet and exercise program and lose the weight, thus changing her label, or she could keep going to interviews until someone saw past her physical appearance and gave her a chance to prove her real worth.

Some other elements that contribute to the makeup of our labels, such as age, race, religion and sex, don't lend themselves to the former option. I couldn't offer any strategies for changing these aspects of your label, even if you asked me to. And I don't have the remedy for the societal dyslexia that causes some people to misread and overemphasize personal flaws and their importance to product's (that's you) performance.

Some people spend their entire lives fighting the barriers created by speech impediments, educational gaps, accents and cultural differences.

But I'm convinced that by recognizing the existence and effect of our labels, as Lupe and Harold have done, we can take steps to control them, and even circumvent our buyers' prejudices.

One important way to do this, thereby giving the product a chance to perform, is with innovative packaging.

#2. *Avoid The Plain Brown Wrapper*

I hurt my neck a few years ago and the injury resulted in some chronic problems for me. So, as you might expect, I've spent quite a bit of time with quite a few doctors. But, to tell you the truth, I doubt whether I could recall any of their names today, except one: Dr. Green.

He wasn't really any better than any of the other physicians I visited, though I thought he was good. But he did manage to make himself memorable. You see, old Doc Green wore the same doctor outfit as all the others guys -- stethoscope, lab coat, bad tie -- but instead of a white lab coat, his coat was green. Get it? He created such a memorable package, how could I forget him?

Your "package," in the context of our product metaphor, is similar to your "label" in that it affects your image and is the result of perception. But while your label is a nearly unconscious name tag created by the subliminal signals that define your "contents," telling the "buyers" in your life what they're getting (is it strained peas, or motor oil?), your package is a thoroughly conscious, highly visible "wrapper" that helps you stand out from all the other products on the shelf. It's your "brand name." (It's not Brand X strained peas, it's *Gerber*. It's not Crazy Eddie's motor oil, it's *Pennzoil*.)

You must be innovative in your packaging if you want to distinguish yourself from everybody else. In other words, you must *be memorable*.

Why is it so important to be memorable? Because, if you aren't remembered, you won't be taken into account. If you aren't taken into account, you won't be bought/selected. In other words, you won't get the raises, promotions, customers, love, recognition, etc. that you deserve -- whether you deserve it or not.

I cannot emphasize enough how important it is to get out there and get noticed! Nowadays it is absolutely critical, especially in the workplace. Why? Because, thanks to the Baby Boom, we are living in one of the most competitive periods in our history. In the 90s there are more people of roughly the same age competing for the same jobs, money and real estate than ever before. And it's going to take more than a red pocket square to stand out in a crowd like that.

Walk down the cereal aisle the next time you're in your local grocery store and take a look at the rows and rows of flakes and pops and cracklin' this and natural that. It's positively mindboggling! Is it any wonder cereal manufacturers spend millions of dollars a year to come up with new strategies to make their products stand out among their competitors?

Well that's us, folks. We're all crammed in together on that shelf, providing a huge selection of products for a limited number of buyers.

But just standing out isn't enough. After all, a large, forearm tattoo of a red skull and crossbones surrounded by the inscription, "Born to Eat Cheese Dip," would do the job. So would a Mohawk, gold teeth and hot pink toreador pants (if you had the caboose to wear them). If all you want to do is to stand out, these strategies should work perfectly, unless you work in a topless bar.

Most of us, however, don't work in topless bars. (If you do, go ahead and skip this section, but pay special attention to the section on "expiration dates.") Most of us have to wear one kind of uniform or another in our workplaces. Salespeople have to wear business suits; cooks have to wear chef's hats; receptionists and secretaries have to wear appropriate attire. Most of us are required to blend into our environments as much as possible; soldiers are actually camouflaged!

Besides, just standing out is never enough. You have to create a package that is not merely memorable, but appealing as well. (Check out those

cereal aisles; not a skull and crossbones in sight --
though the sight of one wouldn't surprise me.)

The good news is it's much easier to control
the design of our packages than it is to manipulate
our labels. A standard tip, for example, for
employees who want to stand out from their co-
workers and put themselves in line for a
promotion has long been this: Dress like those who
currently hold that position. It's simple, but it
works -- to a point. And it doesn't require plastic
surgery or an M.B.A.

But beyond such traditional wisdom, there
are other, and I believe more effective, steps you
can take to create a memorable package. Here are
three strategies that work wonders:

Shop Talk

You don't have to sound like Alister Cooke
or develop a stand-up comedy routine to become a
memorable conversationalist. Just take the time to
develop a strong vocabulary and make sure your
frame of reference is interesting and current. Leave
out the four-letter words and the folksy
colloquialisms. Most top executives never confess
to being "happier than pigs in shit," though I've
run into some line managers with otherwise
promising careers who do. (Don't worry. You
won't be competing with them.) Try to take on the
lexicon of your profession. Listen to your boss and
the higher-ups. Listen to your customers. Take
notes if you have to. This is a very effective way to
package yourself as someone who belongs in a
corner office.

Keep your frame of reference fresh by
keeping up with local news events and generally
maintaining a broad base of interests outside the

office. Read widely and use more than just sports references in your conversations.

Stay informed about your company. Keep your ears open. Read the annual report. Display that extra interest in the goings on at your workplace that sets you apart from the average, put-in-my-eight-hours, take-my-check, and-forget-the-joint workers that surround you. And show that you are knowledgeable and optimistic; none of this, "Good grief! Do you think we'll survive?" stuff. It drives everybody nuts and makes you look like a loser who couldn't find another job if your life depended on it.

More Than a Box

Most of us take our accomplishments for granted. We assume either that they aren't important, or that everybody knows about them already.

This is a fatal mistake that kills a terrific opportunity for personal effectiveness.

Oh, I hear the skeptics: "You gotta be kidding. Who cares whether I'm captain of my bowling team or was voted Den Mother of the Year? My mother's proud of me, sure, but that kind of stuff doesn't have anything to do with my job."

Wrong! Remember: What we're trying to do is design an effective "package," one that is memorable and appealing. We're trying to stand out in a crowd so we won't be lost in the blur of other packages not that different from our own. Our activities and accomplishments outside the workplace present a *perfect* opportunity for this.

EXAMPLE. Jesse was just one middle manager among many middle managers in a large sales and service organization. He worked hard, did his job well and usually met or surpassed his quota each month.

But so did most of his peers. The company was a strong one and it was loaded with talent. Jesse was good at his job and never had to struggle to keep up, but he found few opportunities to demonstrate his own uniqueness.

That is, until he started coaching Little League. Jesse never really thought of his new activity as an "accomplishment," and it certainly didn't have anything to do with work, but he loved it from the moment he hit his first fly ball for fielding practice, and it was that enthusiasm that helped to set him apart from his peers.

Jesse's enthusiasm was so great that it was impossible for him not talk about his team's progress throughout the season. His conversations with his co-workers were always liberally salted with anecdotes about the kids he coached, their parents, other teams and baseball in general. He even kept a team picture framed on his desk, next to the picture of his wife and kids.

It wasn't long before Jesse's co-workers began to ask him how the team was doing. As the end of the season rolled around, even his boss stopped by his desk now and then to check on the team's progress.

Without realizing it, Jesse had become much more *interesting*. By talking about his team at work, he showed that he was much more than just a middle manager. By including his co-workers in the good feelings he had about himself and his "outside" activities, he made it easy for them to feel good about him, too. And, unrelated though it may have seemed at first to his job, his Little League coaching actually made him a more appealing and *memorable* employee to his boss.

Let Your Buyers Be Aware

It's not going to do you any good to create an effective package if your "buyers" never see it. You've got to seek out those persons within your company or group who should notice you and let them do it!

Without knowing it, Jesse applied the principle of product differentiation to his career. He kept himself from being perceived as generic "vanilla" in a freezer case full of other "vanillas." He broke out of his plain, brown wrapper -- and thus went a long way toward eliminating his obscurity within the company ranks.

But this shouldn't come as a serendipitous event, folks. There's no need to wait around for the "buyers" in your life to notice you by accident. Pay attention to the things you do that make you different -- the things that make you *you* -- and let people know about them. If you're a Toastmaster, mention it once in a while at work, invite co-workers to join the club, use your skills as Master of Ceremonies at the company picnic or department meeting. If you were just appointed to the board of directors of your local United Way chapter, let other people in on it, and tell what it means to you and the community. If you ran a 10K race last weekend (it doesn't matter whether or not you won it), speak up!

And most important, begin to live as though your life has been changed for the better by these activities. That way, they will seem worth the effort you are putting into them and you will seem worthy of notice.

And for heaven's sake make sure you are doing things that are worth noticing! Along with your outside activities, your work must always be perceived as high quality and valuable. After all, one of the most effective packages I know is clear plastic over a quality product.

To the uninitiated, this may sound like a clarion call for brown-nosing, but that's only because that's exactly what it is ... Just kidding! I'm not recommending sucking up to anyone. Leave the obsequiousness to Uriah Heep! It's bad for your digestion and most people don't like fawning yes-persons anyway. But I am suggesting that you recognize that there are people around you, in your company and your community, who can reach down and pluck you out of the muck of obscurity. If you want those people to notice you, you have to get their attention.

One sure-fire way to do that is through advertising.

#3.   A Multimedia Approach To Memorability

Now that we've printed our "labels" and wrapped our "products" in memorable "packages" it's time to make sure our buyers hear the good news! It's time for some personal "advertising."

As I've already said in the previous section, it won't help you much to put together an effective package if nobody ever sees it. In other words: It's not just important to do good, your "buyers" also have to hear about the good you do.

So, you've got to advertise. Of course by "advertise" I don't mean to suggest that you should take out an ad in the Wall Street Journal, or don a cowboy hat and ride an elephant before local TV cameras during the midnight movie (cute as you may be in Western Wear). What I am suggesting is that you take a few simple steps to create a personal marketing strategy.

The personal marketing strategy I recommend is what I call a Multimedia Approach to Memorability. It's got a long title, but it's simple -- and effective. It involves the accumulation and display of those concrete, hard-copy items that objectively sell you. Advertising professionals call these items "collateral materials." This term includes such promotional tools used by businesses to market their products as brochures, catalogs and sales letters. It's not hard to see that your personal collateral materials could include, among other things, your business cards, resume, diplomas, positive performance appraisals, or testimonials from satisfied customers.

But our application of this term is necessarily broader than that. Your collection of personal collateral materials should also include items you might not ordinarily think of as "advertising." Jesse's framed picture of his Little League team, for example. Or how about a poster or program from that Girl Scout jamboree you helped to organize; or the newspaper article about that local literacy program in which you taught adults to read. Anything that shows you in a leadership role works best.

And, boy! Do these things work! A thoughtful display of your personal collateral materials on your desk or office walls surrounds you with an aura of individuality and accomplishment. For the buyers in your life who never see more than one side of your personality, these materials put you instantly into a wider context than the narrow confines of your work role. And while they're silently adding dimension to your work persona, they're also serving as concrete evidence of your personal effectiveness.

These materials can provide benefits outside your work environment as well. I've used them myself countless times to help people with "problematical" resumes (a euphemism for having been "fired"), by simply including some choice pieces in the resume package. (Say, a newspaper clipping about some community activity in which the job seeker performed well in a leadership role.) It's still amazing to me just how effective these collateral materials can be. The "buyers" focus on the clipping and, while it doesn't eliminate the resume's negative elements, it enhances the job applicant's image enough to move it beyond the personnel department.

In this way, these pieces can be very effective in helping you switch your career direction.

EXAMPLE. Marsha spent most of her working life as a clinical nurse. (You know: white shoes, white nylons, white hat.) She was a well educated and competent professional who had always enjoyed her work. When she called me for a little career counseling, she had decided on a change. She had decided to get out of clinical nursing and into community-based health education and promotion.

Unfortunately, Marsha was running into an unexpected barrier at every organization she approached.

"Your background is clinical," was a typical response to her inquiries. "Exclusively clinical. What makes you think you can handle fund-raising? Or interface effectively with our board of directors? Or work with our volunteers? Nothing we see in your background really prepares you for anything outside a clinical setting."

Marsha's resume was presenting her as a Nurse Nancy with no flexibility at all.

But Marsha was really a remarkably versatile and adaptable person. (Which makes her situation a wonderful illustration of what's wrong with resumes.) What she needed was an imaginative application of the Multimedia Approach to Memorability.

Our strategy was bold, but simple: We reworked her resume, emphasizing anything in her career and personal life which demonstrated the skills she would need in her new career. And we included a brochure from the local YWCA which was illustrated with a photograph of Marsha leading an aerobics class. It was a truly arresting picture featuring Marsha coaching a room full of attractive women in tights. It showed, too, in concrete terms, that she possessed the flexibility (pardon the pun) and leadership abilities these organizations needed.

That brochure proved to be the magic key into a new career path. In very short order, Marsha's revised personal advertising strategy yielded three job offers.

Sometimes your personal advertising strategy will be very simple, a matter of environmental fine tuning. All you may need to do is create a workspace that reflects you in a positive way. Posting degrees and plaques, as I've suggested, is effective, but you should also consider the overall impression your workspace presents. Ask yourself, "Does my workspace reflect the successful, broad, interesting type of person I would like to know myself?"

EXAMPLE. Lowell had risen to become his company's vice president of corporate communications through hard work and talent. Unfortunately, just over a month after he moved into his new office, his new peers began to doubt the wisdom of his promotion. His desk was piled with papers. Magazines and newspapers littered his office floor. His files were a secretary's nightmare. His walls were utterly bare and his one, frail, dying asparagus fern looked as though it had been cooked in a microwave.

Anyone who met with Lowell in his office received the message his environment was sending loud and clear: *This guy is incompetent.*

But Lowell was not incompetent, his environment was. And he knew if he didn't do something about it fast, his career was going to die a slow, cluttered death. He immediately solicited the services of a professional secretary who reorganized his files. He came in one weekend and eliminated the piles of papers from his desk (and chairs and floor), clearing away years of clutter and really throwing things away for the first time. He organized his workspace so he could readily lay his hands on essential information.

Lowell eliminated ten years of garbage and obsolete materials he had towed along with him as he had moved up the ladder -- materials he was never going to read in the first place. He uncovered a space where he could actually work, and in the process, Lowell uncovered the high-quality professional who had earned that office.

These are just a few of the ways you can use the personal collateral materials we all accumulate.

But even if you decide -- though I don't know why you would -- not to display such concrete evidence of your effectiveness in your work environment, you should still take pains to hang onto it.

Why? Because even if you don't want to show it to anyone else, it still shows *you* what you've accomplished.

I can't tell you how many times I've sat down to help someone with a resume -- his or her personal catalog of accomplishments -- only to hear, "Oh, geez, I haven't really done much of anything with my life. I have no accomplishments."

Bull-oney! We all have accomplishments. The problem is, most of us have hideously short memories when it comes to our day-to-day achievements. After the banquet ends, if we leave without the program in which our names were printed, we forget we had anything to do with it. If we don't save our performance appraisals, we remember that we got the raise, but we don't remember why. If we lose that letter from the Mayor thanking us for helping with the parks cleanup program, we never think about it again.

I recommend keeping a portfolio of personal collateral materials for two reasons: First, it's that concrete proof of your personal effectiveness I've been talking about. And second, when things go wrong -- as they inevitably do -- looking through such a portfolio can be incredibly encouraging. When you think you've hit bottom, these collateral pieces can be silent little cheerleaders, encouraging you just when you need it the most.

The Business Card "Acid Test"

One of the most commonly used personal collateral pieces is a business card; or I should say,

74

misused. The way I see so many people blithely circulating ratty, marked-up, inaccurate, out-dated business cards, oblivious to the harm they are doing to themselves is a tragedy.

Local execs who do a lot of business across the Pacific tell me that when a Japanese businessman is handed a business card, he doesn't jam it into his shirt pocket without looking at it. He cradles it in both hands and takes a moment to contemplate it. He does this because, in his culture, a business card is an important representation of the *self* of the person whose name is on it and worthy of great respect.

I'd be surprised to see an American businessperson pause to contemplate the significance of your business card. But it does make a more important impression than most of us think. The following rules of thumb should insure that that impression is a good one:

A. *Never Write On Your Business Card.*

Inked-in phone numbers, addresses or, God forbid, company names say, "This guy is not prepared." It looks like you've been in business for about a week. It says you aren't ready to do business, and that's the last thing you want to say.

B. *It Should Never Take More Than A Few Seconds To Find Your Card.*

Store your cards in a convenient place on your person. Don't stuff them into your purse or briefcase. Have them handy. If you have to search for one, you look like a loser.

C. *Never Apologize For Your Card.*

Believe it or not, that's what people do most of the time. As they hand it over, they're saying things like, "I'm no longer with this company," or "This isn't my name anymore," or "This isn't the color I wanted." What do they want people to do with such information? The best approach, even if the card isn't just right, is to hand it over and shut up.

#4. *Conduct Ongoing Product Research*
The world is changing.

"So," you might ask, "What else is new?"

What's new is this: The world is changing so rapidly it's almost impossible to believe! Computers, medicine, communication, transportation, space exploration; what was science fiction to our parents has become science fact in less than a generation. Eastern Europe, Asia, South America: who could have predicted the changes now taking place in those regions just five years ago?

We're living in a veritable maelstrom of change! Human knowledge is increasing exponentially. The more we know, the faster we learn more. And it's unlikely this pace will be slowing in the near future. You might be surprised to learn that 80 percent of all the scientists who ever lived are alive today. (Unfortunately, so are most of the politicians.)

And we all know, either quantitatively or viscerally, that the workplace is changing. The job environments we worked in even a few years ago are not the same as the realm we labor in today. The technology is different, but so are the people and so are their attitudes. Gone is the "Company Man," that great American icon -- depicted for prime time by the likes of Hugh Beaumont (you remember *The Beav's* dad) and Robert Young (the father who knew best) -- that married, white male who worked all his life for the same company. The workers of the 90s face a fluid, multiracial, multicultural environment populated equally by men and women. And that average American worker will have three different careers by age 45.

So how do we cope with these gale-force winds of change without losing our hats -- or our heads? With ongoing product research.

Ongoing product research is really a fundamental and genuine commitment to lifelong learning. Nowadays, continuing education is not just a good idea for self improvement or career advancement, it's probably the only hope most of us have of staying employed.

EXAMPLE. James left his home in the Philippines and emigrated to the United States during the 1960s. He spoke no English. But he was a hard worker, and his determination to succeed in his new homeland eventually paid off. Though he spoke only Tagalog, his native tongue, upon his arrival James forced himself to speak only English, constantly listening and asking questions in the unfamiliar language while he worked at his job in a large spice manufacturing operation. He confronted and overcame the language barrier, as well as the cultural barriers, that could have held him back. And in the process James proved to be invaluable to his employers.

But, as they say, nothing stays the same. Eventually, the operation at the old spice factory began to change with the times and technology. Computers were more in evidence everyday as the company shifted to more modern management and production techniques and automated operations. As his workplace became more and more complicated, James felt himself falling further and further behind.

Why? Because, though James had learned to speak English, he had never learned to *read* it -- or any other language for that matter.

As is the case with most successful illiterate adults, James had managed brilliantly to sidestep his handicap in numerous, clever ways. He never seemed to have his glasses. He listened to the radio and watched television to keep up with the news. He was a master of interpreting photographs. No one but his own family knew his secret.

But James knew it. And he also knew that with computers becoming such an integral part of his company's operation, his secret would soon be discovered.

So, at age 50, he finally confronted his illiteracy. He enrolled in an evening adult reading program. He took a step that opened vast new areas in both his professional and private life.

James is a wonderfully practical example of someone who conducted ongoing "product research." The "product," again, was James himself. His "research" was his awareness of the changes around him, both of his environment (the spice factory) and of those who operated successfully in that environment. His research showed him that, if he was going to continue to be bought/selected in his new environment, he was going to have to adapt to those changes.

Ongoing learning keeps us fresh and involved in the predictable changes that move us forward, and it keeps us fit and ready for the unexpected changes that could leave us behind.

A high school diploma, for example, used to be all most people really needed to start their working lives equal to their peers. After they completed the twelfth grade, they could get good jobs, buy homes and support their families. College was education beyond the norm and it moved you into a distinctly higher job arena.

Today, a college degree is much more basic, and that higher job arena is peopled with those with advanced and professional degrees.

But, though I am certainly an enthusiastic advocate of higher education, that's not necessarily the form your ongoing product research needs to take. Even nascent Ph.D.s must face the fact their knowledge is becoming obsolete almost as soon as they acquire it.

In fact, your ongoing product research needn't take place in a classroom at all. The idea here is to expose yourself to new things and new people and to constantly look for new opportunities for personal growth.

EXAMPLE. Jesse, the middle manager/Little League coach cited earlier (see how easy he is to remember?) confessed to me that he learned as much working with young ball players as he did in a community college course on management. He learned practical lessons about leadership, how to motivate, and how to cope with a dual role (parent and coach). He grew from the experience and found he was less surprised by changes in his company and better prepared to adapt to those changes.

If you make a genuine commitment to lifelong learning, you will find yourself learning from all kinds of sources: bosses, co-workers, spouses, clubs, even television (though I include the *idiot box* with strong reservations).

Don't hide from the classroom, either. Universities, community colleges, professional organizations -- even your own company -- all offer seminars and one-day courses that you should be sampling.

You don't have to learn it all. Even if you wanted to, you couldn't. But you have to be awake enough to see that "it" is not the same "it" today as yesterday, nor will "it" be the same "it" tomorrow. Invest in some research and development and your product will never become obsolete.

#5. *Know Your Competition*

Sachel Paige once said, "Don't look back; something might be gaining on you." Well I hate to disagree with one of the Boys of Summer, but I say: Go ahead, look over your shoulder. In fact, look over both shoulders! Look up, look down, look all around. Something is gaining on you, folks. It's the *competition*.

That's why you are conducting your ongoing "product research." You must keep a weather eye out for your competitors. Fortunately, they won't be hard to spot. They're everywhere: down the street, at a rival company, across the Pacific, in Japan, two feet away, sitting in the next cubicle. In a workforce full to overflowing with Baby Boomers, they're practically standing right there in your loafers with you.

But those "others" are only one aspect of the competition we all face, no matter what our education or profession. Our ongoing product research will help us to keep them clearly in sight, but our toughest competition of all is even closer, though for many of us, he's a lot harder to spot.

But I'll show him to you. Take a break right now and go into your bathroom (bring the book). Now walk up to the sink and lean real close to the mirror. There he is! You are now facing the toughest competition you will ever face.

Your *real* competition in your life isn't the latest Harvard MBA or Stanford graduate to hit the job market. (Not that those kinds of qualifications aren't useful, and not that you couldn't acquire them yourself if you were so inclined.) But if the concept of "competition" is to be meaningful at all, it must really begin with the *self*.

So, in the spirit of knowing your competition, I recommend asking yourself the following questions:

If I Were Suddenly Promoted or Laid Off, Would I Be Ready for My Next Position?

You must be ready to move ahead or move on from wherever you are now in your career development or you are going to be left behind. Don't make the mistake of thinking, "I've made it. Now I can sit back and enjoy it." Don't you believe it!

And don't make the mistake of thinking your job is secure. Companies fail -- good, established companies -- all the time. Products and services become obsolete. There are layoffs and cutbacks and reorganizations afoot every minute.

One of the fastest growing industries in the country today is the so-called "outplacement" industry, whose bread and butter is sudden unemployment. Whether you wear a blue collar to work or a Brooks Brother's suit, there is no such thing as job security.

Am I Trying to Be the Best I Can Be?

How do you really compare with your peers? Your superiors? Your subordinates? Are the young guys coming onto the company payroll better educated than you are? Do they have more to offer than you do?

One of the best things about worrying about the competition is that it shakes us out of our complacency. I don't think it's a particularly good idea to worry obsessively about the other guy knocking us out of the running. Most of us can't afford to spare the energy it takes to fret about such things. But a little concern about that other guy is healthy. It puts things into perspective.

Take the time throughout your life for regular personal inventories. Look at your educational level, your work experience, your age. Ask yourself how you stack up against others in your position in your company, as well as the industry as a whole. Examine your progress. Are you standing still? If you are, you can bet your track shoes someone's gaining on you.

If There Were Someone Right Behind Me, Would I Be Doing Exactly What I'm Doing Right Now?

Your answer to this question can tell you a great deal about how you're really doing. If you've stopped putting out, you're going to be put out to pasture. It sounds cruel, even unfair, but those are the rules, fair or not. Disapproving of them is one thing, ignoring them is another.

And are they really so unfair? Is it fair for the rest of us to have to drag the deadwood? Is it fair for those who have unconsciously given up to weigh down the rest of us?

The fairest situation is one in which effort and excellence is rewarded. (You must think so too or you wouldn't be reading this book.)

#6.   *Support Your Price*

Here's another question: What's your price?

"Well, let's see ... Last year I pulled down about 35K. But that's not counting 'bennies' and the company car. And then there's the condo Dad left me, and the Volvo's still pretty new, and then there's my savings..."

No, no, no ... The question isn't, "What's your current net worth?" It's "What's your *"price."* (And I don't mean what would you take to throw the big game.)   In other words, what would a potential buyer be willing to pay for your time, your efforts, your attention, your skills, your talents, etc. -- in short, *you?*

Now that you've determined your "label," designed your "package" and developed your "advertising" strategy, your next step is to determine what to charge your "buyers." If you've conducted your ongoing "product research," you should have a pretty good idea of what you're "product" is worth within its market, as well as just how it stacks up against its competition.

Now ... Are you worth that 35K-plus-bennies-plus-company-car you're pulling down?   Really worth it?   Would you be offered that level of compensation if you entered your particular job market today? If the company instituted cutbacks, would you be among those deemed worth keeping?

This "price" question is always a tricky one, because market factors do have a tremendous influence. Independent contractors --- plumbers, physicians and consultants like me -- usually have more experience with this sort of thing than most people. We're used to standing up and declaring our prices to our buyers. We're used to being pinched and prodded like melons in a fruit stand. And we're used to being compared to the other melons in the pile.

But most people are more accustomed to lining up and sorting offers. So, to many, the question becomes, "What will the market allow?"

But there is a much more revealing angle from which to examine this "price" concept, both for independent contractors and salaried employees. Instead of, "What's your price?" ask yourself this question: "What am I doing to support my price?"

So many people feel that showing up, punching in, slogging through the day and then punching out again is all it takes to earn their price tags. They have an I'm-not-giving-more-than-I-get attitude about their jobs (and often their relationships as well). They feel that anyone who puts themselves out, stays at his desk after 5:00 or gives a hoot about his job is a sucker.

But to support your price -- that is, to be worth your paycheck or the investment of trust or affection your "buyers" have made in you -- your product must offer *value*. And that means you have to give more than you get.

It's never been enough to just do your job. Employers think of their workers' salaries as investments. And we all want the greatest possible return on our investments. The employees that are considered the most valuable investments are the ones providing the greatest yield.

I don't mean to say that the only workers who are considered valuable by their employers are the workaholics of the world who put in 70-hour weeks, take work home every night and come into the office on weekends. More often than not, value can be found in simple things.

EXAMPLE. Jan was the newest secretary at a medium-sized software development firm. Her job was mainly filing and typing letters and reports. She worked closely with other secretaries in the firm and also with one particularly harried marketing director.

One day, the marketing director flew past her desk, dropping off his latest report for typing as he did. Usually, he proofread all of his own reports once they were typed. In fact, he had made a point of telling Jan when she started the job that she was never to edit anything he had written. She was simply to type, that was her job.

But today the marketing director was late for an important meeting and the report had to be on the boss's desk by 5:00.

"Just type it up and send it over," he said. And out the door he went.

When Jan sat down to type the report, she was immediately struck by some odd figures. She had worked closely enough with the marketing director to notice that these were not the numbers he had been talking about all month.

"Hey," a co-worker told her when she asked him for advice, "don't worry about it. Old ants-in-his-pants told you not to mess with his stuff. Type it, send it over and forget it. That's what I'd do."

Jan, however, did nothing of the kind. Instead, she searched through some notes on the marketing director's desk and found the figures she believed were correct. Then, she typed up two copies of the report, one with the new numbers.

By the time the reports were finished, it was nearly 5:00. So she checked the marketing director's schedule, found where he had gone and interrupted his meeting.

He was angry as he picked up the phone, but, when Jan read him the numbers he had left for her, his anger turned into shock and then, when she told him of her alternate report, relief.

Jan remained a secretary for exactly one year. She's since been promoted to research assistant to the marketing director.

That's *value*. Jan was no workaholic. She just cared about doing a good job. She supported her price by giving value. She gave the same kind of value to her husband and her children as well. Jan wasn't just a valuable employee, she was a valuable person. She gave her "buyers" more than their money's worth.

And remember, anyone who is not satisfied with giving his employer their money's worth might as well forget about raises or promotions. Why should anyone pay you more if you're not worth more?

By now you probably feel as though you've been grilled on the witness stand by Perry Mason, but I've still got one, final question for you about your "price": What are you worth to *yourself?*

You have a heck of a lot invested in your *you*/product and you have to take the responsibility for managing that investment if you want it to continue to yield a high return.

What sorts of things are you doing to make yourself more valuable?

Are you spending money on yourself to update your "package"? Looking after your wardrobe? Having your hair styled? Or letting it go gray?

Are you spending the money to keep yourself looking vital? Joining a health club? Letting your stomach bulge? Are you staying fit so that the next 22-year-old hotshot who walks through the door isn't automatically more attractive, fit and energetic than you are? (Hey, that was more than one question!)

The period between ages 40 and 55 is the critical coasting phase for most of us. I don't know if we just start to tire out, or if, in this youth oriented society, we just feel that we are no longer worth the investment.

But you *deserve* to spend money on yourself to make yourself a better, more effective person. You are incredibly valuable and you are worth it. If you don't see that, no one else will either.

#7. *Live Your Warranty*

Remember the last time you came home from the mall with, say, a portable tape deck you had picked up on sale? Remember how great you felt about getting such a great sounding unit for such a good price? Remember how you wanted to kill somebody when it started to eat your tapes?

"Well," your sister said, "I guess you get what you pay for. You didn't think they'd be on sale if they were worth anything, did you?" (Didn't you feel like killing *her?*)

Were you inspired to shop at that store again? No, of course not. You felt ripped off.

But then you noticed that the tape deck had a *warranty.* A warranty is a promise that a product will do what it's supposed to do or the manufacturer will fix it without charge. And that's

87

only fair. After all, the manufacturer promised that the tape deck would play the tapes, not eat them. If you'd known your irreplaceable, bootleg *Rolling Stones at Altamont* cassette was going to be turned into magnetized iron oxide confetti, you wouldn't have slipped it trustingly into your new deck.

What this means for us within the context of our "product" metaphor is that you, as a "product," have made a promise to your "buyers," as well. You have promised that you can do what you say you can do and are worth what you say you are worth.

But if you're not, you have the right to get fixed. Personally effective people have fantastic warranties. Because they know they are valuable products, they know that a glich here and there need not be fatal. If a personally effective person runs into, say, some aspect of her job that she didn't expect and doesn't have the skills for, she gets retrofitted. She plugs into the things she needs now that she didn't need when she was originally selected by going to a local community college or by requesting special training. Just as she takes responsibility for all other aspects of her "productness," she accepts her warranty as well.

She's never passive. She takes a proactive approach to her warranty. If her problems become more than she can handle, she gets professional help. Drug and alcohol abuse, for example, cost employers millions of dollars every year. Yet many employers have company-sponsored recovery programs.

Everybody has problems. It's all right to have problems; it's not all right to leave them unattended.

#8.   *Know Your Expiration Date*

I met a woman at the gym the other day named Ida. She was a pleasant person and we got along well, so I did what I inevitably do, and asked her about herself. She told me that she lived nearby and she was a teacher's aide in a local school.

"That's interesting," I said. "How long have you been doing that?"

"Twenty years," she said, offhandedly.

"Wow!" I said. "Twenty years. Have you ever thought about becoming a teacher?"

"Oh yes," she said. "And if I decide I'm going to stay in this business, I'm going to go back and get my teaching credential."

Life, as they say, is what happens when you're not looking.

While my new friend was deciding what she was going to do, about half of her working life had passed her by! I'm not saying that she couldn't still go out and become a teacher. I hope she does and I wish her well in any case. But she really and truly amazes me, nonetheless. Why do people think they can wait until later to live their lives?

This may seem like a grim note on which to end this chapter, but let's face it folks, none of us is getting out of this alive. And that's not just a cute crack, either. This offer *expires* sooner than you think. Unless we are aware of the realities of time passing, we labor under a misconception that is one of the surest threats to our personal effectiveness.

It's not just death I'm talking about. Nothing lasts forever. Even if your company has a long and fruitful life, you still have to retire someday. Parenting has an expiration date, too. It's true that once you're a parent, you will always be a parent, but kids don't stay kids forever. They really are gone before you know it.

But back to death. While all of us will feel its sting sooner or later, some of us seem bound and determined to feel it sooner. For that surprisingly large segment of the population that takes its health for granted, all of it -- kids, home, job -- could be gone in a heartbeat.

EXAMPLE. Larry was a settled and well-established realtor when he experienced what Dick Leider calls a "wake-up call." After years of struggle, he had built his firm into one of the most successful operations in his region. He was fat (both his figure and his financial statement) and happy, with a routine life virtually free of the risk with which it had been fraught in his early years.

One winter, he and his wife, Helen, and their friends, Arthur and Millie, traveled to Hawaii for a two-week vacation. The foursome had been friends for more years than they could remember, and they often vacationed together.

They had barely unpacked their bags at their beach-front hotel when Arthur decided to go for a jog on the beach. Larry said he'd meet him by the water.

Less than a minute after he started running along the warm, blue water, while his wife continued to load two week's worth of clothes into a hotel dresser, Arthur collapsed on the sand. By the time Larry arrived, he was dead.

His friend's heart attack affected Larry deeply. It shattered several unconscious assumptions about his own life. It showed him in graphic terms that our time is limited.

After the funeral, Larry went to his doctor for a physical, closed down his real estate office and opened a small, country store he and Helen had talked about since they were newlyweds.

"It's something I always meant to do," Larry told me. "I figured it was now or never."

We can't live our lives as though they are going to go on forever. No one is *that* personally effective. And even though more and more people are living into their 80s, 90s -- even well over 100 -- we won't be *working* much past 60. The time to look after your health, invest in your education, change your career, is *now*. So what if you'll be 40 by the time you graduate, you'll be 40 anyway. And you can't say you've been overweight your whole life, your life is not over -- yet.

Joan Baez said it best: "You don't get to choose how you are going to die or when. You can only decide how you are going to live, now."

6

REACHING OUT
TO HELP YOURSELF

If you broke your ankle, would you set it yourself? Dumb question! After the initial screaming had subsided, you'd hobble down to your local emergency room and kick back while the doctors and nurses took X-rays, served painkillers and wrapped you up in quick-drying plaster.

What if you were accused of income tax evasion? Would you represent yourself at your trial? Of course you wouldn't! You'd find yourself a good tax lawyer and (after the initial screaming had subsided) hand him all your records and pray.

And I'd bet the farm that in either of the above situations you wouldn't think twice before reaching out for help with your problem.

But what if your problem wasn't a medical or legal one? What if, say, you couldn't seem to dress appropriately for your profession? Or your accent was so thick you had a hard time doing business over the telephone? Or you were angry all the time for no apparent reason? Or your husband had Alzheimer's disease and you spent nearly every waking moment caring for him until you felt ready for a nervous breakdown?

What then? Would you look for outside help? What kind of help would you look for?

Where would you find it? How would you know if it was any good? What if you needed ongoing help? How would you get it? Buy it? Manage it?

This book is about becoming personally effective, and it's chock full of strategies employed by some very effective individuals toward that end. But, hey, nobody is *perfect!* Even the most effective people in the world have problems they lack the resources or expertise to solve on their own.

But having problems is no problem for personally effective people because they employ one of the greatest personal effectiveness strategies of all: They give themselves *permission* to have problems; permission to be inadequate in certain areas; permission to be broken.

And, most important, they give themselves permission to get fixed. They sometimes flounder, but never for long, because they know that it's not just other people who deserve help. They know that reaching out for help is sometimes one of the most effective moves they can make.

Unfortunately, whenever I talk to people about reaching out to help themselves, I run into sarcastic comments like this:

"Yeah, Brigid, sounds great. Just hire an expert to solve all your problems. Sign me up!"

Of course, no one can solve all our problems, and I'm not suggesting that anyone can. What I am saying is that we can't solve all of them ourselves, either. I'm saying it's foolish and costly to pretend we can. And I'm saying that the most effective thing we can do when we're up against it is admit it, look for a helping hand and get on with our lives.

FOUR REASONS TO REACH OUT

There are probably as many reasons for seeking help from professional service providers as there are problems to be solved. But here are four of the most important ones:

#1. *To Save Time*

Every year, right around the first week of April, Herb went into a panic. Tax time! Year after year he swore he'd be ready, he vowed to beat the deadline. And every year he ended up filing for an extension, and then another one, until he found himself in some pretty deep doo-doo. Then, just as he managed to extricate himself, it was tax time again!

You see, Herb was one of those people who felt he should do his own taxes. He was a competent manager. He handled budgets, expense statements, quotas, inventories. Why couldn't he handle his own taxes?

Why? Because Herb didn't have enough time! One of the reasons he was a good at his job was that he worked very hard at it. How could he possibly keep up with all of the changes in the tax code? And since he was successful -- high salary, owned his own home, kids in college -- understanding the intricacies of that mercurial tax code was absolutely essential. What Herb didn't know always hurt him.

Herb was certainly a smart guy who could have learned to prepare his own taxes. But unless he quit his job and devoted all his time to it, he would always be a beginner.

We're all smart guys who could learn to do hundreds of things -- if we only had the time. But personally effective people recognize this absolute time limitation without letting it limit their effectiveness.

How? They reach out and use the expertise of others.

#2. *When You Can't Do It Yourself*

Ana was also a competent manager. Though she had only recently been promoted to a supervisory position when I first met her, she was already wowing them down at the home office. She seemed to be able to accomplish things that were utterly beyond her predecessor. There seemed, in fact, to be nothing Ana couldn't handle efficiently and effectively.

Ana wasn't really more talented or intelligent than the guy who did the job before her. Ana simply knew something he didn't: She knew what she could do, and she knew how to find people who could do what she couldn't.

Ana's predecessor thought he had to do everything, from designing his staff's workspace to doing his group's own publicity. And that killed his effectiveness, because nobody is good at everything.

Ana realized that some of the tasks for which she was responsible were actually different businesses from the one she was in, requiring expertise she lacked. What did she know about interior design? What did she know about cultivating relationships with media people or formatting press releases?

Nothing, that's what. But Ana knew that her lack of expertise in those areas needn't hinder her. She knew that the most effective thing she could do was reach out.

#3. *When The Opportunity Cost Is Too High*

Common sense tells us that there are only so many hours in a day and whenever we choose to do one thing, we are, in effect, choosing *not* to do another thing. If I choose to work 16 hours a day, for example, I'm also choosing not to spend time with my family. If I choose to keep my home as clean as Beaver Cleaver's mom even though I work full-time, I'm also choosing not to do anything but housework on weekends.

These are examples of *oportunity cost* -- the opportunity to do one thing you give up in order to do another. Everything we do has this kind of price tag. There's no escape from it. Watch television; you don't read. Work late; you miss your daughter's play. Walk into Cinema I; you miss what's playing at Cinema II.

Personally effective people recognize the inevitability of opportunity costs, and they recognize that they have a choice in the matter. They know that when the opportunity cost of being all things to all people gets to be too high, it's time to reach out.

Personally effective people also recognize another cost of doing it all yourself that goes beyond any individual service provider's fees: *The cost of doing it wrong.*

EXAMPLE. Munson and his wife, Alison, decided to sell their own home. Munson was being transferred by his company to another state and they thought selling the house themselves was a great way to avoid paying middleman fees. They immersed themselves in real estate lore, analyzed the entire market and acted as their own agents. But selling a house these days is no simple matter. One wrong move and the deal is blown.

And that's exactly what happened to Munson and Alison. After months of open houses and individual showings -- months of keeping the house continuously spotless -- they finally found a buyer. But at the closing, a misunderstanding about the points to be paid nearly scotched the transaction. Because their moving date was looming they were desperate to rid themselves of their house. So they paid the points and sold the place for thousands less than they had expected.

What they gave up in terms of stress, time and, in the end, money, hardly compensated for those "middleman fees."

#4. *To Reward Yourself*

Up to now, I've cited only solid, sensible, Protestant-work-ethic type reasons for reaching out for help. But there's another reason that is, in my view, just as important as all the others. Sometimes we should reach out and avail ourselves of the services of experts simply because we want to. Just as personally effective people know we all deserve to get fixed when we're broken, we also recognize the importance of plain old indulgence. We work hard, we deserve to be rewarded. We deserve a massage, biofeedback therapy or six weeks of NutriSystem; whatever works as a positive reward for *us*.

Of course, what is one person's indulgence is very often another person's necessity.

EXAMPLE. Joel had always done his own laundry and cleaned his own house. He was a single guy with a fairly large hunk of free time available during the week, so he was able to do a pretty good job. But he hated it. In fact, the very thought of his weekly cleaning chores gave him a headache. So one day, he said to hell with it and hired a housekeeper.

Diane, on the other hand, was a single, working mother with two kids to raise. Her choices were simple, clean the house or sleep. Her decision to hire a weekly cleaning service was hardly an indulgence.

But what if it were? Joel's decision to hire a housekeeper made him happy, eliminated a source of stress and improved his standard of living. In other words, *it made him more effective.*

And that's something we all deserve.

TYPES OF SERVICES

The services I'm talking about reaching out to in this chapter are professional services. Traditionally, the expression "professional" referred mainly to lawyers, physicians and accountants. But I prefer a much broader definition. In the context of this chapter, a "professional" is any person who makes his or her living by performing his or her service and takes that job seriously. There are professional housekeepers, massage therapists, manicurists -- I've even known professional waitresses.

For our purposes, these types of professional services fall roughly into two categories: *needs* and *wants.*

#1. *Needs*

One of my favorite sayings is: "A need met; a problem solved." I can't remember where I heard it, but whoever said it, said a lot. You see, when we feel needy, we can't be effective. It's that simple. It's human nature. If you've got an emotional hole somewhere, all of your personal effectiveness is going to leak right through it.

EXAMPLE. Elizabeth was about 40 years old when she first came to see me for career counseling. She hadn't worked for quite a while and she said she needed some help getting back into the job market.

"But before we get into any career counseling," she said as she pulled up a chair in my office, "there's something very important you should know about me."

"Okay," I said.

"Well," she continued, "I was married right out of high school, but my husband died within a year and a half of the ceremony and I've been a widow for 23 years."

"To tell you the truth," I told her, "this is the first time I've ever met anyone who made that particular situation into a career. Are you telling me that you are a widow by definition?"

"No," she said, obviously unhappy with my seemingly unsympathetic response to her revelation. "I'm a widow by circumstance."

"Yeah, but 20 years? You're probably better at that than you ever were at being married. The fact is, you've become a professional widow!"

Needless to say, our first meeting didn't turn out the way either of us expected. But to Elizabeth's credit, she didn't back down. She was determined to climb out of the incredible hole she had dug herself into. She was in no way ready for my services, but there were plenty of other counselors out there who could help her.

Clearly, Elizabeth *needed* to reach out for help. She had fallen below a fundamental *baseline* of personal effectiveness. It's not a hard line, and it varies with the individual, but you can always tell when someone has dropped below it. That's when relationships crumble, health deteriorates and jobs are lost.

The types of personal service providers that fall into the category of *needs* are those who help to bring you up to this fundamental baseline. Psychologists, marriage counselors and special support groups like Alcoholics Anonymous are a few examples.

In fact, I'll bet you can't name a personal problem, addiction or family dysfunction for which there isn't a solid support group in this country. They've risen over the years out of the ashes of unfulfilled needs. And they work.

Elizabeth ended up visiting a grief counselor who helped her to understand the role she had defined for herself and how she could change it. She reached out, found the solution to her problem and went on from there. In fact, she actually started dating.

Unfortunately, there is a strong element of denial inherent in these kinds of problems. Consequently, those who need these kinds of services the most are often the least likely to look for them.

Sometimes our own needs are masked by the needs of other people in our lives.

EXAMPLE. Stanley and Rose had been happily married for over 30 years when they learned that Rose had Alzheimer's disease. Neither of them really understood what was waiting for them down the road. But as his wife's health declined, Stanley found that he was as much a victim of the disease as she was.

Rose eventually required 24-hour-a-day care. Stanley loved his wife and he rarely left her side. But after a while, his love turned to resentment, and as he felt more and more trapped, virtually unable to leave their apartment for even an hour, his feelings began to sour toward hatred.

Then Stanley heard about a service called *respite*. Respite care is one of the fastest growing services for those caring for the elderly or chronically ill. A respite worker steps in to relieve the family member who serves as the primary care giver. Often the service just takes the burden for a couple of hours, but for people like Stanley, that couple of hours makes all the difference in the world. By reaching out to this service, Stanley found the relief he needed, and kept the love for his wife intact.

Counselors and social service types aren't the only service providers who satisfy needs. Certified financial planners, for example, have special expertise in a wide range of financial products and services to help people with life-long personal economic goals.

This may at first appear to be something other than a need. But folks, money in today's society is rarely anything but. And most of us don't have the time or expertise to even begin to understand our options in this area.

Look off into the distance for just a moment, off to where most of us are heading when we retire. How are we going to survive when we get there? There are so many people in this country living for the moment, not taking the time to plan their futures. Medical technology is lengthening our lifespan almost as fast as the federal government is spending our Social Security fund. How we use our money now during our peak earning years -- how we invest it -- will determine whether most of us enjoy our declining years or live on a street corner out of a shopping cart. Needs don't get much more basic than that.

#2. *Wants*

Needs are basic requirements, passing grades, so to speak. But sometimes just passing isn't enough. You may *need* a "C" to pass, but you *want* an "A."

I occasionally hear people make statements like, "You shouldn't want that." Or, "You don't need that. Why do you want it?"

I admit that I'm confused by such statements. Within the bounds of common sense and decency (whatever that is) how can one person possibly know what another person should or shouldn't want?

Still, people are much more likely to give themselves permission to reach out for needs than wants. But a truly effective person, sooner or later, says to him or herself, "Hey! I deserve this!" And that's the bottom line.

Let's say you go to work in an environment in which you must dress professionally. That means, for men, that you must wear a suit and tie, and, for women, an appropriate business ensemble.

Sounds relatively easy. You buy a suit. You buy a tie. All set. Right? Wrong!

Implicit in your new dress code is the idea that you will not only wear appropriate clothes, but that you will put them together competently. Your tie must go with your suit; your shoes must go with your handbag.

Suddenly you discover, Hey! This ain't easy! Men are much better off in this arena since, unlike their female counterparts, they can get by forever on the basics. But even that is too much for some people. Dressing well, for men and women, is something that takes practice, maybe even talent. And dressing well, studies show, definitely helps you to be more effective; to move toward your "A."

But who has the time to scour the magazines and keep up with the ever-shifting demands of fashion? Or maybe you just don't have the knack for dressing smartly. Maybe you just don't like it.

So, what do you do? Do you continue to be perceived by your peers and supervisors as a nerd? Or do you reach out and become more effective?

If you're smart -- and you must be since you bought this book -- you reach out. But you don't go to your sister, or your husband for this kind of help. You go to a professional; a personal shopper. This service is sometimes provided by individuals (John T. Molloy, the author of *Dress For Success* is in this business), but more often by clothing stores anxious to attract your business.

Here's how this service works: Your personal shopper gets to know you, your taste, your comfort zone, your income, what you already have hanging in your closet and what you need or want to add. Then, the shopper helps you pick out your clothes.

Personally effective people use this kind of service because they want to be more than "C" students. They are unwilling to let their own inadequacies hold them back. It's not a sin, after all, to not know how to dress well. It's not your fault. You don't know what you don't know. But it's sinful, indeed, to waste your time and money doing it wrong.

Here's another example: Women certainly have a tough row to hoe in the world of business, but it's not easy for men, either. Male executives are expected to be youthful, strong and vigorous. And those expectations have become more pronounced in the last few years.

But what older male execs tell me is that, no matter how vigorous they actually are, they must be *perceived,* to be so. They must maintain a youthful image. Their jowls and shiny heads haven't actually affected their talent or intelligence, but others still believe them to be less effective.

That's why many older execs, facing what is clearly age discrimination, are fighting back. But not with lawsuits. Instead they are going to their doctors for male-pattern baldness treatments and facelifts.

Other common ways people address their wants:

● **Adults getting teeth straightened.** "Mom and Dad couldn't afford it, but that doesn't mean I have to live with this snaggle-toothed grin forever."

● **Speech coaches.** "An Austrian accent may work for Arnold Schwarzenegger, but it makes me sound like Colonel Klink." Or: "I'm bright, talented, hard-working, but my speech impediment makes me sound incompetent."

● **Errand runners.** "I'm tired of trying to be Supermom! And all this running around is diminishing my effectiveness on the job and at home."

● **Massage.** "My wife is just as tired as I am at the end of the week. Begging her to rub my back is creating lots of stress and resentment around here. But I deserve a back rub!" Make an appointment together.

● **Housekeepers.** "I've got two days off a week. I can spend it with my family, or I can spend it scrubbing toilets."

Remember, these people are not servants. They are professional people selling you a service. Hiring them is what they want you to do. Their work, while unattractive or untenable for you, is their livelihood.

And you don't have to be rich to afford these services. You have to make choices. If you want the cleaning team to come in once a week, you might have to give up going out to lunch every day. You might have to make a few sacrifices, but you don't have to forego your wants.

FINDING THE RIGHT PERSONAL SERVICE FOR YOU

Utilizing personal services starts with self-awareness. If you can define your problem, you can probably find a group or service to address it.

But that's not always easy. Sometimes one of the hardest things to do is put our finger on just exactly what our problem is *called*. And if I don't know what it's called, how can I reach out?

If, for example, I want my teeth straightened, it's obvious that I need to call a orthodontist. Or if I'm overweight, there are dozens of weight loss organizations all around me. But where do I go if I'm depressed? Who do I call if I'm not having satisfying relationships with my spouse, children or co-workers? Where do I turn if I hate my job? Do I go to a marriage counselor? Or some other kind of therapist? Should I talk to my priest or my rabbi? Maybe I should I just add fiber to my diet ....

To complicate matters, there's usually a certain urgency at work when we begin to look for personal service providers. The decision to look for help is precipitated by some kind of crisis. We usually become aware of our problem or need through some kind of negative feedback. Most of us don't even think about going on a diet until we can't get our zippers up. Some of us have to get fired before we realize we have an attitude problem. And some unresolved problems can bubble to the surface suddenly and unexpectedly like an erupting volcano.

Typically, when people begin looking for information about personal service providers, they go to one of three places:
1) friends/families,
2) religious organizations or
3) human resources departments at work.

Unfortunately, these are the last places they should look. A much better starting place is one you might not think of:

The Yellow Pages. You'll find a number of headings you can look under for service providers, such as Emergency/Crisis; Addictive Behavior, Information and Treatment; or general Community Access pages.

But more important, your phone book provides a list of information and referral agencies. (This is a service for the services!) Information and referral agencies don't offer, say, legal help, but they do know who does. Most have information about locations, fees and can possibly refer you to other information and referral groups. Colleges also have information referral services. There's a person down at most city halls who does nothing but answer off-the-wall and not-so-off-the-wall inquires about services available in the community. These people are sometimes called *citizen advisors.*

And don't forget the information desk at the public library.

And here we come to one of the greatest problems we face when choosing social services. There are far more excellent social services out there than there are excellent spokepersons for them. These people often do a wonderful job, but they are not marketing oriented. They often provide services they simply cannot articulate to the public. So, people don't find out about them. When I talk to day-care associations, the number one problem they tell me their members are facing today is lack of customers. Lack of customers? In the middle of a day-care crisis? You bet. The services are out there, but sometimes you'll have to dig for them.

There's another resource that's readily available to you as you begin to reach out to become more effective: Someone you know who has solved the same problem. Just walk up and ask. What could be easier? Yet many of us are reluctant to try this. Who wants to ask someone how they kept their rotten marriage together?

But, remember, you are asking someone who no longer has the problem. People who have gotten help and have moved on are usually very willing to help others.

In fact, if you think about it, you're giving that person quite a compliment. You are saying, "Hey, Ralph. You seem like you've got it together. I'm not together myself. How'd you do it?" Or, "Gosh, Gloria, you're a terrific dresser. I could use some help myself. How do you do it?"

Now you might find out that Gloria reads ten fashion magazines a week. Okay, she does it on her own. But she's still plugged in and might offer some suggestions as to where you could look next. She might suggest some services I haven't even mentioned.

But whatever you do, as you begin to reach out, don't assume that all of the effective people around got that way on their own. It's a sure bet they had to reach out at one time or another, too.

THE BOTTOM LINE

So you've identified your need or problem. You've found some service providers. Now, you're probably wondering, how do I know they're any good? How do I know they're worth their fees? And once I've bought the service, how do I manage it and make sure I'm getting what I paid for?

As with any product or service you buy, you have to look at purchasing personal services from a consumer's point of view. In other words, shop around, kick a few tires, make comparisons.

Then, take a close look at the following checklist for buying and managing a personal service.

#1. *Can I Afford This?*

This seems like a reasonable place to start, but it's amazing how often people fail to ask themselves this question. I think one reason for this is that by the time we finally get around to reaching out for help we've actually *needed* it for an awfully long time. We're so needy that our judgment is clouded.

You have to make sure you can afford the services you are seeking or you'll create more problems than you solve.

You might also want to ask yourself the above question in another form: What is this service worth to me? The answer may be: A hell of a lot. It may be worth making some sacrifices in other areas to provide relief in this problematic one.

Be careful to establish some kind of price ceiling when you engage a service. People are stunned when they tell a service provider, "Go ahead, whatever it takes," and then get socked later with a huge bill. Beware: People *will* take advantage of you if you let them. Don't go into this feeling helpless. You're the customer; you're in the driver's seat.

#2. *Ask For References*

Ask lots of questions: How long has this provider been doing this? Who else is satisfied with this service? What "brand" names can this provider drop? Anyone you know? Individuals or organizations of prominence in the community? Ask for names, get phone numbers and call people.

Some types of service providers aren't going to be able to give you phone numbers. Clients of a clinical psychologists, for example, probably wouldn't be too happy to hear from you. But all personal service providers should have some kind of references that you can check independently. Any who don't should be avoided.

#3. *Be Specific About What You Are Buying*

Be specific and don't be intimidated. These folks are experts at what they do, but it's up to you to make sure that what they do is what you're looking for.

Here's what I mean: Clearly a personal shopper is there to help you dress better. But how much better? Do you want to look like a model from *GQ?* Or are you shooting for the look of an effective, but conservative, middle manager?

Or maybe you've hired a housekeeper. Do you want him/her to dust everything, or just the furniture in the communal areas of the house? Is he/she going to do the laundry? Wash the dishes? Make the beds? Brush the dog? Spell it out; everyone will be happier.

#4. Establish The Parameters of The Service Delivery

Good, experienced personal service providers have spent years helping many people with needs or problems such as yours. But everyone's situation is unique. We all have jobs, families and other responsibilities that have to be dealt with, too. It's up to you to make sure your service provider understands the limits of time, etc. under which you operate.

Say you go in for regular massage therapy, but the masseuse routinely starts 15 minutes late and then adds a half hour on the end to make up for it. That could create incredible scheduling problems. That service provider may think she's giving you a great deal, but you have to make sure she understands that she's screwing up your day.

Or maybe you've hired a wardrobe consultant who recommends items that are far above your budget category or that would make you inappropriately overdressed for your profession. Again, it's up to you to clue this person in. If a service provider is good, he or she will undoubtedly hone in on your particular needs, but, remember "professional" is not synonymous with "mind reader."

#5. *Know What It Looks Like Fixed*

By the time most of us reach out to personal service providers, we are very needy. We've probably been in the situation we're trying to change for some time and it may not be easy to see how things *ought* to be. But it is essential that we give this a great deal of thought. It's the only way we are going to know if the service is working -- or not.

#6. *Let Them Do It*

Believe it or not, this is a really tough one for some people. A surprising number of people hire a personal service provider, and then do everything they can to keep them from doing their job. I can't tell you how many cleaning people have told me they quit a job because the person who hired them insisted on working side-by-side with them. This drove them nuts! And I know a wardrobe consultant who is constantly confronted by people who say, "Hey, I don't wear green. I don't wear jackets. I don't wear belts. I don't wear hats."

Well, folks, that's why you're there in the first place. While it is essential that you take an active role in managing the services you buy, does it make any sense to keep the professionals from providing it?

Remember, if these people are any good, they are going to push you, challenge you, help you to move forward. They are not going to say, "Whatever you want. You're the customer." If they do, you are absolutely *not* getting your money's worth, whatever you're paying.

In fact, effective counseling by its very nature is going to make you uncomfortable. Sometimes you just have to stand back and hang in there for a while.

#7.   *Is It Working?*

This question isn't as tough to answer as you might think. If you've taken the time to determine what you need and how your problem would look fixed, you should have a good idea of how your service provider is doing.

Sure, she's the wardrobe consultant and you still think it's improper to wear socks without a hat, but you can see how people are reacting to your new look. Has anyone made any comments? Do they seem to like it? Ask a few people.

Sure, he's the counselor, but you know whether you're feeling more excited and empowered. How do you feel? Are you making progress?

Maybe your problem was that you were spending your weekends cleaning your house instead of enjoying your family. Well? Is your house clean and are you spending time with your family?

Common sense is your best ally. Always keep the lines of communication open between you and the service provider. How can the housekeeper know she's supposed to beat the rugs if you never mention it? If you've been going to a therapist for one week and you haven't shown any improvement, maybe it's because it's a six-week program.

Be sure to tell them when you are dissatisfied. Be specific: *This is half of what I expected; I thought such-and-such was part of the deal.*

Also, tell them when you are happy with things. You are relying on your service providers' skills and expertise, but they are human, too, and all of us need a pat on the back once in a while. Use your best people management skills. They, and your providers, will serve you well.

EXERCISE FOR CHAPTER SIX

Undoubtedly the Chapter got your creative juices flowing. Now go ahead and use your active imagination to identify areas where you *need* or *want* help to increase your personal effectiveness.

<u>NEEDS</u>

1.

2.

3.

4.

5.

6.

<u>WANTS</u>

1.

2.

3.

4.

5.

6.

7

CREATING AND MAINTAINING EFFECTIVE AND SATISFYING RELATIONSHIPS

For some reason I have never been able to fully understand, the subject of managing strategic relationships is a touchy one for many people.

"It's using people," many people snort. "I'm not the kind of fake, manipulative mercenary who makes friends with someone just because that person can help my career. And I'm not some smarmy butt-kisser who sucks up to the boss to make brownie points toward a promotion either!"

Really? You mean to say you've never joined the Jaycees, a local Rotary Club or some other service organization to network and make business contacts?

"No, never."

You've never gone to an office party to get better acquainted with your supervisor?

"Uh, no."

You've never called up someone you don't know very well who has some expertise in your field and asked for a little advice?

"Well, I..."

Maybe if we take the subject out of the cold, cruel business world for just a moment, into, say, the slightly more warm and fuzzy world of the arts...

Imagine for a moment that you are a young artist, a painter. You've attended a good art school and you are out in the world trying to make a living. But nobody has heard of you yet, so, to pay the rent, you've taken a job doing paste-up work for the local newspaper. But your heart belongs to the brush, the canvas and your own special vision of the world.

On your day off, you visit a gallery where a well-known local artist is showing his work. It's wonderful! You have admired this artist for some time now, but this is surely his best work to date. The artist himself is making an appearance today and you decide to introduce yourself. You tell him how much you admire his work and you mention that you are a painter yourself. He likes you and expresses interest and, before you know it, you are asking his advice and he is giving you tips and a relationship is born -- a *strategic relationship*.

A LEG UP

All personally effective people cultivate and maintain strategic professional relationships.

Why? Because the fact is, some of us have achieved more than others. There are people out there who have already achieved, right now, what we hope to achieve someday ourselves: fame, fortune, education, artistic status. And, let's not mince words here, there are people out there who are more important than we are; people who have access to knowledge, resources, jobs, experiences (cabins on Lake Tahoe) that we don't have. Building strategic relationships with those people isn't just a shortcut to the top, it's one of the most important keys to personal effectiveness.

I'm not suggesting that you go out and begin manufacturing inauthentic relationships just so you can get ahead in business. Far from it. All effective strategic relationships are, by their very nature, reciprocal, *quid pro quo* situations.

What I *am* suggesting is that you pay attention to your professional relationships and take an active role in making them work for you.

In this chapter we will be looking at several strategies for building and maintaining effective, strategic professional relationships. But first, a question: What exactly are professional relationships? And, even more important: What's the difference between a professional relationship and a personal one?

PROS AND PALS

While it's certainly possible to develop personal friendships on the job, and while it's also true that personal friends often contribute to our professional development, there are some tremendously important differences between personal and professional relationships.

There are three essential elements that must be present in our personal relationships that are not (or should not be) present in our professional relationships:

1.   Shared interests and values.
2.   Shared vulnerability.
3.   Shared support.

Shared, as you can guess, is the operative word here. Most of us have had a personal relationship in which we did all the work; *we* made the lunch dates; *we* confided our innermost secrets;

we cancelled that hot date on Saturday night with that incredible law student to eat a gallon of Haagen Daas in a dorm room and talk about her latest breakup all night. (Of course, as soon as *she* had a hot date she dropped you like a hot rock.)

These kinds of personal relationships are anything but effective. All of the above elements must be present in order for a personal relationship to be truly satisfying to both parties. In other words, if you're not sharing the load, you're getting the shaft.

Personal relationships in which all of the support, all of the interest and all of the initiative comes from only one side will inevitably fail.

You can't build an effective personal relationship on common misery, though I know dozens of people who try. People who meet each other at work and hate the boss together, or unite against the boredom of their jobs, don't have enough of a foundation on which to build a friendship. They're like drunks or cokeheads who have only their addictions in common.

The very ingredients that combine so compatibly to form the firm foundation of a solid personal relationship will eat away at the structure of a professional relationship like termites in a woodpile. The same openness and vulnerability -- the same sharing -- is absolute death when applied in a professional environment.

In other words, professional relationships must include a rather high level of *containment*. Remember, anything you say can and will be used against you in a professional relationship. Whether we do it deliberately or unconsciously, we store all the information we get from each other in our work and professional environments, racking up a score. If the information you give me says, simply, "I'm competent and professional," that's good, comforting news for both of us. You've *contained* all that stuff about your abortion and failed marriages.

If you begin to offer me information of a personal nature, you confuse me -- and that's bad news for both of us. I am no longer sure of my footing when I'm around you, and you have really stepped in it.

EXAMPLE. A shopping mall manager I recently consulted with was terminally confused about the differences between a personal and professional relationship. When I met her for the first time, she spoke clearly, shook my hand firmly and presented herself professionally (sharp suit, calm demeanor, good vocabulary).

Then, not 15 minutes after we met, she asked me this incomprehensible question: "Tell me something, Brigid, do you think I ought to have a baby through invitro fertilization?"

I was utterly at a loss for words -- a rare event for me. How on earth could I know whether this virtual stranger should have a test-tube baby? Why would I care? Why would she choose to muddle things up this way? What kind of a flake was I working with?

As it turned out, the shopping mall manager wasn't a flake, but a highly competent business-person. Unfortunately, she continued to saddle our relationship with all kinds of inappropriate personal revelations that decreased her effective-ness -- and nearly drove me nuts.

Another, more general, example of this kind of confusion is something I call *The Walton's Syndrome.* It's the We're-A-Happy-Family policy that's popular with some companies. It manifests itself in company sports teams, Friday afternoon barbecues, beer bashes and parent/child relationships between the executive staff and its workforce.

If you currently work in, or ever expect to work in a company suffering from The Waltons Syndrome, listen carefully, John Boy: No matter how much you may like your job or the people you work with, *your company is not your family.* That any company would lie to its employees in this way is puzzling to me; that any employee would fall for this kind of rubbish is downright astonishing.

I honestly believe people are happier and more comfortable in a professional environment free of this kind of nonsense. There needs to be a balance in the workplace between distance and empathy. How else is anybody going to get any work done?

If you want your relationships to be effective and satisfying, you must be able to recognize which types they are. What I hope I'm communicating here is that you must develop and manage *both* for personal effectiveness.

TYPES OF PROFESSIONAL RELATIONSHIPS

There are two types of people with whom we have professional relationships: *maintainers* and *propellers.*

#1. Maintainers

The maintainers are people who can make us or break us. There are three kinds of maintainers, the first are the "keystone," or "core" people, such as secretaries, administrative assistants and waiters. These are the people who do the job when we aren't around. How we treat them determines whether they are part of an effective support network, or a constant source of aggravation.

"Experts" are the second type of maintainers. This group includes our colleagues, professional contacts and others whom we respect and value -- people off of whom we can bounce ideas.

The third type of maintainer is the "tangential helper." These include subcontractors who, while not necessarily doing our jobs, take on essential tasks that make our jobs possible.

#2. Propellers

There are two types of propellers: "mentors" and "role models." Mentors are the hands-on folks who guide us and help us with opportunities and access. Role models are our heroes, people we will likely never meet, such as Abraham Lincoln, Gloria Steinem or Mark Twain.

SEVEN STEPS TO DEVELOPING STRATEGIC PROFESSIONAL RELATIONSHIPS

Personal relationships grow out of our basic psychological needs; professional relationships grow out of our goals. While *most* people handle their personal relationships effectively (I emphasize "most"), a surprising number of people have no idea how to cultivate and maintain the kinds of long-term professional relationships that are essential to achieving their goals.

The following steps provide guidelines for developing and managing these essential relationships.

#1. *Do Your Homework*

There are all kinds of people out there who are richer, wiser and more powerful than you are. But only of few of those people are really important to you *strategically*.

Few would argue for instance, that Donald Trump, Lee Iaccoca and T. Boone Pickens are rich and powerful individuals (though I'm sure their wisdom is in doubt in some circles). But how much could any of these men help the young artist in our earlier, hypothetical example with his goals and aspirations? I suppose any one of them could sponsor him, or buy some of his paintings. But how much useful career advice could they give? What tricks of the trade could they offer?

And, anyway, how likely is it that the young artist would ever have access to any of those guys in the first place?

Not very. But that's okay, he doesn't really need them. Our young artist can find plenty of strategic relationships right in his own backyard -- and so can you. But you've got to do your homework.

First, ask yourself who are the people who are strategically important to you? Are they young or old? Men or women? Peers or mentors? Are they in your community? Or in a local trade association or service organization?

Ask yourself how much time you have available to devote to outside commitments and what type of activities you actually like. Investigate the various groups and activities in your area that might present opportunities to meet people who are strategically important to you.

And look for something outside your field of expertise, outside your comfort zone. If you are an accountant, for example, don't expect to get much mileage out of a membership in your regional accounting association; you already know enough accountants. But if you join a local chapter of, say, Toastmasters, you are bound to meet people from a very different quarter of the community.

Also, don't just go for the brand names. Just because Dear Old Dad was an Elk, doesn't mean you will shine in that organization. Get involved in something you really want to be involved in; it's the only way you'll be effective in that activity, anyway.

The idea here is to get out in the open, look good, and meet people.

#2.   Gain Third-Party Support

Third-party support is the endorsement or sponsorship of those people who can give you a boost into an organization, club, job -- whatever -- in which you are interested. Here are six strategies for gaining this kind of endorsement:

Ask for It

I'm surprised at how many people balk at the idea of making a simple, direct request for support. It's honest, straightforward and about as manipulative as voting.

But to make it work, you've got to be specific.

"Brigid, I'm going to interview for this new PR job next week. You've seen me perform well as the publicity chairman for the United Way. Could you write a letter documenting my accomplishments?"

It's even more effective to write up a list of those accomplishments yourself. Or, better still, write the letter yourself. If you're not specific, you'll get something that says you're a great person who is easy to work with, when you *need* mention of the three television spots you produced.

Remember: This is not a personal relationship where we are best buddies and anything I write will be okay by you. You need a specific recommendation. Besides, the more specific you are, the better people like it. If you ask for a general endorsement, people feel you are asking them to take on your whole life.

Let Them Off the Hook

You can't have an effective strategic relationship unless you are willing to receive all kinds of information, both good and bad. When you try to gain third-party support, you are going to someone who knows something about you and whom you hope will want to recommend you.

Maybe they *don't* want to recommend you. You need to know this and you need to let that person feel free to let you know: "Bob, you are in a position to know the level of effort we put into this project. It's important to me to document that. It's important that someone like you make that kind of endorsement. What I'd like to do is draft a letter and have you sign it. But if there's anything in the letter that makes you feel uncomfortable, or you feel should be deleted, or if for any reason you don't share that sentiment, you need to tell me."

Whew! I know it's scary, but when you approach third-party support this way, two things happen: 1) you let your potential supporter off the hook, which makes them feel better and gives you greater credibility, and 2) you can get some amazing feedback.

Make It Easy for Them
   That's what you do when you draft the letter of recommendation. Offer to get them the phone numbers or addresses they need. Do whatever you can to make it *easy* for them to give you their support.

Express Your Appreciation
   Sometimes (more often than you might imagine) people aren't aware of the roles in which we see them. It's important to articulate what you see to those you seek support from: "I'm asking for your endorsement because you are the premier bank president in town." *Who? Me?*

Report Back
   This is absolutely the most crucial step. If, for example, you ask to use someone as a reference on your resume, call back and let them know that you got the job. But whether you get the job or not, *call back.* This, more than anything else you do, is what helps to create the trust and involvement that makes the relationship work.
   Remember: Many people in these kinds of influential positions tend to feel used by others much of the time. This step is what makes the difference between calling on somebody with whom you have a strategic relationship and using them.

Send Thanks
   This differs from reporting back, which usually takes the form of a phone call. Send those who have supported you a personal note of thanks. Tell them, in writing, what they did for you and what it has meant to you. Reporting back is a

touch; sending thanks is concrete documentation that validates the value of their efforts on your behalf.

And, again, remember: The higher up the social and economic ladder you are, the less likely you are to receive a thank-you letter. It means a lot.

#3. *Participate in Social Engagements*

Social gatherings are golden opportunities to network and begin building effective professional relationships. Don't pass them up!

Often when I speak at all-day conferences I notice that, though most people will attend the prescribed program from 9 to 12, they disappear at lunch, only to return when the program resumes at 1:30. What a huge mistake these people are making! Here they are, attending a conference to meet other people and they evaporate at the first sign of a non-structured environment.

Folks, you've got to work the room! You can't sit in the corner with your group of six and expect to get the kind of contact that will generate professional relationships. Reach out to other people. Establish yourself as a presence in the room. And really make the event a good time for everyone.

I recently listened to another consultant who was speaking on this very topic. Something she said has stuck with me:

"The most important thing you can do at a social engagement is to walk up to someone and *pretend* you're interested."

The reason that stuck in my mind is that it is one of the most cynical recommendations I've ever heard, and I think it told us more about the speaker than it did about being effective in social gatherings.

I believe you must be *genuinely* interested in others, and really care about them having a good time, to be truly effective in this environment. It's just something you can't fake.

#4. *Be a Resource*
People constantly ask me, "Brigid, besides yourself, who's a good speaker who could address our organization?" Every chance I get, I endorse those persons in whom I have confidence. I don't feel threatened because I know that creating opportunities for other people really pays off for me in the end.

Whenever you can provide introductions or leads for others, you become a resource. And, far from costing you anything, it demonstrates your *access power* (see Chapter Ten). It shows people that you are someone who is connected, knowledgeable -- and it cements your professional relationships with those you recommend.

Also, the good things you say about someone else say good things about you. They say that you can recognize someone else's competence, and they say that you are good enough that you are not threatened by such recommendations. And, if you say that someone is honest, you are also saying that honesty is something you value, and people will infer that you are honest, too.

Effective people don't have to have the spotlight always shining on them to look effective. Shining a little light on someone else is one important way to maintain your existing professional relationships, and create new ones.

#5. *Offer Assistance and Help on a Professional Level*

This is a tough one, and you may flinch when you read it, but, if done properly, offering comments and criticism of colleagues is an essential part of developing and maintaining effective professional relationships.

First: Always frame your comments in professional terms, offering assistance and help. Second: Always direct your criticism at behavior, not individuals (see Chapter Three).

I can give you a fairly innocuous example of what I'm recommending from my own experience. My family recently decided to change dentists. When our old dentist called us to ask why, I could have said just about anything, but I told him the truth: We always had to wait too long for service. I had mentioned it on several occasions and nothing changed, so I took my family's business elsewhere.

He took my comments in the spirit in which I offered them, and, in fact, told me that they were money in the bank for his practice.

An example that's not quite as innocuous is that of a co-worker with an alcohol or drug dependency problem that begins to manifest itself in the workplace. If you say anything, they are going to hate your guts -- until they get help. Then they will remember that you were the one who intervened while everyone else stood by. You were the one who valued the relationship enough to step in.

I know that people always shoot the messenger, but this is not only an opportunity to strengthen a professional relationship, it is your responsibility.

#6. *Seeking Advice and Counsel*

This isn't a pathetic, on-your-knees, go-to-the shrine, you-know-everything-tell-me-how-to-live-my-life type of effort. This is what is commonly called information interviewing, and you can do it with almost anybody.

My favorite example of the effectiveness of seeking advice and counsel can be seen with recent college graduates or people making career changes. There are thousands and thousands of occupational titles in the job market. Most of us know about seven. As the aforementioned two groups set out into uncharted waters, they can set a safer and quicker course with a few calls to those in the know.

EXAMPLE. An overworked RN named Sara decided she was sick of the role she'd been playing, the hours she'd been working and the pay she'd been getting. She wanted a change, but she had no idea how her skills could transfer into other areas. So Sara proactively sought the advice and counsel of educators and businesspeople in her community. Nearly all of the people she contacted were helpful, and together they smoothed her transition into another field.

#7. *Seek Opportunities to Demonstrate Your Capabilities*

Ask yourself: What is it I'm good at and how can I show people? You can't just do the work and hope people will notice. You have to look for opportunities *to be noticed* by those people with whom you can and should have professional relationships.

This does involve some risk, but it's worth it. Here are two examples of people who looked for opportunities of this sort and reaped the rewards of their initiatives:

I once consulted with a shopping mall which precipitously lost its leasing agent. There were leases in the works and there were leads dangling on businesses needing space.

The company's marketing secretary had close and frequent contact with the leasing agent and, though she didn't have his experience, she was familiar with the job. So, when she offered to take over the spot temporarily, upper management was delighted.

She was very good at sorting out the details and getting the leasors to agree to the standard lease wording, and she got help with the things which needed to be negotiated. She insisted on sitting in on those negotiations, and, at night, she studied for her real estate license.

By the time the mall's managers got around to hiring the leasing agent's replacement, the marketing secretary had her license and had proved her abilities -- so she also had the leasing agent job.

When a spice company I'd worked with called upon its employees to help out with the company Christmas party, one of the administrative assistants stepped forward with the idea of putting together a special blend of peppercorns and having them custom wrapped for the employees as favors. The bosses loved the idea, and the administrative assistant managed to complete the project on time, within budget, using only in-house help.

He not only demonstrated his ability to get the job done, he demonstrated his influence in the company by getting a number of different departments to help him with the project.

Because our lives are so jammed nowadays, we are constantly ranking the relative importance of our relationships. It's unavoidable, and the level of your personal effectiveness depends on how well you manage these relationships.

Always remember that there is a child in each of us, and that child needs to have fun! He needs to let his hair down, ventilate, swear and act goofy once in a while. If you fill your life with grim, *scheduled relationships*, you'll find yourself missing the spontaneity personal relationships offer.

While your personal effectiveness in large measure depends on how well you manage your professional relationships, don't work so hard on that aspect of your life that you neglect the rest. To be truly effective, you must have both professional and personal relationships that satisfy your needs as a human being.

8

STRESS MANAGEMENT STRATEGIES THAT WORK

Most of the news about stress is bad: It's bad for our hearts and it's bad for our heads; it's bad for our careers and it's bad for our families; it's bad for you; it's bad for me; it's bad, bad, *bad!*

Well, here's some good news about stress: If we understand it -- and through that understanding, manage it -- stress can be an extremely powerful and positive force in our lives.

Back over in the bad-news column, however, is the unfortunate fact that most of us never take the time to learn enough about stress to understand it. Most of us prefer to line up and grab onto the latest stress management fad, clinging to it desperately like rows of parking lot pennants while stress buffets us like a cold winter wind.

But, folks, it doesn't have to be that way! Stress is not inherently good or bad. Gravity, for example, is one of the most stressful forces in nature (just ask my bathroom scale). Wouldn't it be ludicrous to describe the force that keeps everything on this planet from floating out to meet the Voyager space probe as either good or bad stress?

In fact, some events most of us would consider to be good ("You got the promotion!") are just as stressful as events we would consider to be bad ("You're fired!").

And have you ever considered the kind of stress you were under at the time of your own birth? Finding yourself suddenly yanked (and I mean yanked!) from a quiet, warm, cozy place where your every need was met on demand and thrust into this cold, uncooperative world is one of the most stressful events you, or any other living being, will ever experience.

So, I ask you, what could be more natural than stress?

Of course, you might argue, there are unnatural levels of stress. And, you might say, there are unnatural applications of it, too.

Agreed! A remarkable number of the people I work with behave like stress junkies. They almost seem to get high on tight deadlines and impending disasters. And if they don't have enough stress in their lives to satisfy this destructive habit, they actually create *more* of it.

I know retailers, for example, who wait until a week before Thanksgiving to hire their temporary Christmas help. Rather than planning ahead, interviewing and training, they prefer to leave their livelihoods in the hands of disinterested strangers who don't know the inventory and couldn't care less. I know working parents, both men and women, who never include the details of raising their children in their daily plans and, so, find themselves suddenly without baby sitters or forced to choose between attending an important business meeting or the school play. I know property managers, people who are in a business that is usually pretty routine and not particularly stressful, who ignore problem tenants until they are forced to evict them.

Needless to say, these are not examples of positive uses of stress. These are examples of people who are not using stress in ways that will help them to become more personally effective. What they are doing is turning up their stress thermostats without looking at their thermometers -- and that just makes things hotter.

THE FIVE STRESS TRUTHS

You can avoid spending your days toiling in a veritable hothouse of stress by taking some time to examine the dial on your stress thermostat. If you look closely, you'll find five settings which I call The Five Stress Truths:

#1.   *Stress is Inescapable*

Stress, in all its myriad forms, is an integral part of life. We can mitigate its negative effects. We can modify it, often control it. But eliminate it? Impossible!

But we still try.

It's amazing to me the number of people who say they are trying to avoid stress by choosing not to work. The fact is, next to secretaries, housewives are one of the most highly-stressed groups in our society. It's a career with no financial reward, no status and a never-ending workload. Talk about stress!

Also, many seniors expect to make their escape from stress when they finally get their gold watch and leave the world of work forever. Yet studies show that the single most stressful situation most of us will ever face is retirement. In fact, a significant number of people actually *die* one to two years after their retirement date.

Often the strategies that we employ to solve our stress problems are as stressful as the problems themselves. The stress that must be endured by the children of a bad marriage is certainly awful. The fights, the tension, the feeling that it's somehow their fault. The stress that follows them after the divorce is no less formidable. Now they must deal with new boyfriends and girlfriends, possibly stepparents and stepsiblings. Not to mention visitation hassles. And, of course, the guilt is often still present.

A new mother returning to work who has found reliable, professional child care for her baby has allegedly eliminated her worries about managing her job and her family. One kind of stress replaces another as the guilt, expense and harrowing logistics take their toll -- not to mention feeling that she has abandoned her child.

#2.   *Stress is Personal*

In other words, something that might throw you for a loop, I might not even notice. Something that might really drag me down, might just roll off your back.

EXAMPLE. Marla, a business executive I once worked with, stands out in my memory as a perfect example of the extremely personal nature of stress. She was a highly successful district manager who appeared at first to be the most imperturbable woman I had ever met. Her ability to stay cool under pressure was legendary in her company. Her ability to design and implement effective management programs had brought her praise and promotions; she now had 17 local operations managers reporting to her.

And yet, this tough, intelligent, hard-working woman could be reduced to tears by almost any negative personal remark. Bring Marla an impossible deadline, a devastating cutback, a wrenching schedule change; she was calm as ice. But tell her she was not well-liked by her employees; Marla melted.

Another example of the personal nature of stress can be seen in a company I worked with during a workforce transition. The firm had decided to move a huge number of its customer service people from what were essentially clerical positions to sales positions.

Some of those workers responded to the change this way: "You know, I've been with this company for 17 years and the workplace is constantly changing. This is just one more change. No big deal."

But other employees reacted like this: "I've been with this company for 17 years and how do they repay my loyalty? By forcing me to do something I don't like and am not good at. I'm not even sure I believe in it! The only thing I can do is leave. But where would I go? I've never worked anywhere else."

Would you be surprised to learn that the company's absenteeism rate shot through the roof?

Physical stress is also very personal in nature. Some of us are easily stressed by health problems, while others of us don't seem to notice.

It's this very personal nature of stress which makes it so difficult sometimes for us to understand each other.

"Geez, Harv, lighten up, willya? It's not the end of the world. It's just a misdirected requisition form. It's not like the World Series was cancelled.

One man's meat is another man's poison. While the other guy is digging into his Quarter Pounder, you're turning green and gasping for air. Is it any wonder it's so difficult to get others on our team when something is bothering us? If they don't understand that we are actually experiencing stress, they'll just ask us to pass the fries. That lack of understanding is one of the things that makes a stressful situation worse.

And it's the reason one of the most important keys to successful stress management is first determining *our own true sources of stress*, and then dealing with those sources, rather than concerning ourselves with what other people think we ought to find stressful.

#3.   *Stress is Cyclic*

Grandma always used to say, things come in threes. Well, she was right -- only sometimes they come in tens! I can best describe the cyclic nature of stress with this phrase: Stress breeds stress.

Commit this to memory right now: *Stress breeds stress.*

Just as any assault on our systems -- a cold or the flu, for example -- breaks down our physical resistance, so stress breaks down our emotional defenses. As our defenses are weakened, smaller setbacks create greater impact -- until the most innocuous bit of friction can feel like an industrial beltsander.

EXAMPLE. Kevin, an executive with a large company on the East Coast, was precipitously laid off from a position he had held for nearly ten years.

He didn't sit around the house, drinking beer and swearing at his kids, but the extremely high level of stress he was feeling was clear to his family.

So clear that they began feeling it, too. Not long after the layoff, Kevin's wife, a strikingly fit and active woman, became chronically ill, and his kids, both normally good students, began getting into trouble at school.

You see, stress is contagious. Kevin's reaction to being laid off created more stress and it spread to his family almost immediately.

Kevin broke the cycle of stress by taking a family "time-out." Nobody had really been aware of what was happening. But when they took a moment to recognize their situation, they saw that Kevin's wife and children were seeing only the negative side of the stress he was feeling. They couldn't see that he was taking steps to find a job and manage one of the most stressful events of his life. He had developed a concrete plan, he was seeking outplacement counseling, contacting headhunters and developing resumes. His family was unaware of what he was doing to solve the problem. They saw only that he was a debilitated, scared and upset Dad. Once they saw that he was fighting back, much of the stress soon dissipated.

One of the most important things to remember about stress is that as your level of stress increases, your ability to cope with additional stress decreases. So, when you are under a lot of stress, you must be prepared to assume a more defensive position. You need to do something you probably don't do much of in your hectic life: You need to say, "No." And you need to say it until your tongue bleeds.

#4. *Stress Can Dramatically Influence Behavior*

Have you ever watched the Olympics? Well, millions of other people have watched right along with you as the world's athletes step into starting blocks, climb up to diving boards and leap onto parallel bars. We've all watched together as those athletes -- some of whom have worked and sacrificed for years toward this moment -- take their one shot at the history books.

Talk about stress! Olympic competitors eat it for breakfast in the mornings and brush their teeth with it at night. Yet they still manage to set lifetime bests and world records -- because they are using stress to positively influence their behavior, to propel themselves toward success.

In my work as a consultant, I see people every day who achieve equally impressive successes in the workplace. These are people who face enormous challenges and yet beat the deadlines and surpass expectations.

Both these Olympic athletes competing on tracks and in gymnasiums before millions of onlookers and these workers striving for excellence in obscurity are grappling with incredible stress. But each group also has clear, achievable goals. So, the stress they encounter as they strive toward those goals is influencing their behavior in very *positive* ways.

Their behavior is contagious. People around them, their teammates and co-workers, begin to feel very *positively* stressed and very positively motivated. The pressure is still there, of course, but it's shared. It becomes the very vehicle through which teamwork and genuine synergy are achieved (neither of which would be there without it).

Stress can also influence behavior in negative ways. In situations where people are faced with truly devastating reverses in either their professional or personal lives, stress can drive them to do highly uncharacteristic things. Things they would otherwise condemn.

EXAMPLE. Ted was an assembler at a mid-sized electronic design and manufacturing firm. He was a friendly, easygoing individual who rarely lost his temper for any reason. He always dealt with his bosses and co-workers with the kind of equanimity and patience that made him very popular around the plant. So popular, in fact, he was eventually promoted to a supervisory position.

But for all his hard work and goodwill, Ted had very little management training. He lacked the skills, education and experience his new position required. His new responsibilities created a tremendous amount of stress in his life, and his reaction surprised everyone.

In a matter of weeks, Ted was using his new found power in an astonishing number of negative ways. Without the proper tools to ply his new trade, he began to flail at his employees with the tools he did have. He used sarcasm to criticize behavior; he showed blatant favoritism; and he adopted a punative attitude toward some of the support staff. All in his effort to show his bosses "his stuff." As Career Track speaker Kare Anderson once said, "If the only tool you have is a hammer, pretty soon, everyone looks like a nail."

Ted effectively spread his own stress around his section of the plant until his bosses began to feel it, too. Eventually, they recognized that his need for training was the source of the stress and they stepped in to provide it for him. His improvement thereafter was dramatic and it wasn't long before he was de-Hitler-ized. But the experience cost him a lot of friends.

#5. *Stress Can Be An Asset Or a Liability*
When I'm training outside salespeople, I like to take some time to talk to them informally whenever I can. When I am able to do this I inevitably hear statements like this:

"I'm going to be making this call on Wednesday that will really make my month -- if I can land the account."

Or this:

"I've been going after this account for months and I'm finally going to pitch the deal to the real decision makers tomorrow morning. It's got to go well or I've wasted six months."

I hear similar examples of these kinds of do-or-die statements from engineers, middle managers, executives -- even CEOs. (I even hear them from my own children.)

It's easy to see that these people are under a great deal of stress. But it's not as easy to say whether it is an asset or a liability. Some people are able to funnel their performance stress and anxiety into positive energy that gets them off their duffs and into action.

For others, this level of stress is paralyzing.

EXAMPLE. During a supervisory effectiveness course I taught at Ted's manufacturing plant, I encountered two newly promoted supervisors whose attitudes about their recent advancement were as different as pizza and oat bran.

Hope was really excited about the class, and she was thrilled about her promotion.

144

"It's the opportunity of a lifetime!" she said. "And the extra money is sure going to come in handy."

Don, on the other hand, hated the whole idea. He had been promoted against his wishes and he felt that the company was setting him up for failure.

"There's not enough money on the planet to compensate me for the friends I'm losing."

Here were two line workers facing the same promotion: virtually the same position, workload, pay increase, responsibility, but their reactions were polar opposites. It's not necessarily what happens to you that causes stress, but your reaction to it.

SOURCES OF STRESS

Now that you have a clearer understanding of the nature of stress, let's take a look at its sources. There are three:

Your Situation

Situational stress comes from events that are beyond our control.

EXAMPLE. You are a renter in an apartment building where the landlord discovers that the building has termites. It's certainly not your fault that the little varmints have chosen your domicile for their culinary activities, but you are going to have to board the cat and vacate the premises while your landlord bombs them into oblivion.

Other People

While situational stress tends to be periodic and transitory, stress from other people tends to be institutionalized and permanent.

EXAMPLE. You don't get along with your supervisor. But then, you never get along with your supervisors. You just don't like authority. If your current supervisor is replaced by a new one, there is still a high probability that you will experience similar stress.

Some people in some roles will always be a source of stress. For some of us, it's our mother-in-law. For others, our stepmother or stepchildren. Regardless of how they play out their roles, you will always see them as sources of stress just because they exist.

Your Mind

The stress from our minds comes from automatic, largely unconscious, habitual patterns of thinking -- what Shad Helmsteddar, in his book, *What Do You Say When You Talk To Yourself,* calls "self-talk." It's a tape of mostly negative comments that plays constantly in our heads: "I'm too fat." "They won't like me." "I can't handle this." "I shouldn't have worn this dress."

Imagine all this self-talk is coming from another person, someone who is beside you constantly throughout the day muttering statements like the above, running you down and shaking your confidence. I think you can see how stress producing that could become, especially when this internal noise conflicts with our external goals.

Burn Out

We've all heard of burn out. We usually hear it with the word "job" in front of it, but you could probably preface it with just about anything; "volunteer burn out," "kid burn out," "marriage burn out," "burger burn out."

People burn out because human beings were not meant to run at full throttle all the time. It seems to work for a little while, but if you accelerate through the atmosphere at light speed, you're surely going to burst into flames -- burning a few of the rest of us along with you. If you're a supervisor, for example, you can scorch your work group. If you are the CEO, you can drag your whole company down in flames.

So, get your fire extinguisher and watch out for the three most common symptoms of burn out:

1. *Hyperactivity With No Depth*

"Yeah, put my name on your stationery, but you'll never see me again."

2. *Involvement At or Near Physical Collapse*

"I'm so busy. I work so hard. I'm so tired."
"You want to be on our committee?"
"Sure!"
"Huh?"

3. *Emotional Bankruptcy*

"I've got nothing for you and I've got nothing for me. I have ceased to feel."

Rust Out

People suffering from rust out aren't moving through the atmosphere fast enough to ignite any fires. In fact, they're not moving at all.

A woman I met at a community social function a while back illustrates this syndrome very well. She was only 25 but she looked 50. Though she used to hold a highly visible and pivotal position in a high-energy organization, she had chucked it about a year earlier for a dull job far below her abilities and experience -- and at about a third of her previous salary. She was using only about a tenth of her powers in a position that had no chance for advancement.

"I just don't want to be somebody anymore," she told me. "I don't want to do anything and I don't want to go anywhere."

When I asked why she had chosen such a dreary road, she confessed that she had done it shortly after she learned she could not have children. After that, she felt the need to be free of stress.

She was free of any stress, all right, but she was rotting from lack of fresh stimulus. She was exhibiting the three symptoms of rust out:

1.   *Apathy*

"If I cared enough to bother, I'd tell you that I just don't care."

2.   *Signs of Clinical Depression*

"The earlier I start my nap, the quicker the day will pass and I can hit the sack."

3.   *Withdrawal*

"Thanks for calling. I can't come to the phone right now, but if you'll just leave your name and message, you'll never hear from me again."

Beep!

NOW YOU KNOW YOUR ABC'S

Dr. Meyer Friedman and Dr. Roy H. Roseman are the well-known cardiologists who conducted a ten-year study of 3,500 healthy San Francisco businessmen between the ages of 30 and

60. The group represented a wide variety of lifestyles, personalities and physical types, and the good doctors were studying them in hopes of uncovering those factors that predispose some individuals to heart disease.

The results of that study changed the way we view heart disease and it added two new phrases to our vocabularies. Today, anytime someone seems to be married to his job, a hard-charger or a workaholic we call him a "Type A." Anyone who seems to be more laid-back and easygoing is definitely a "Type B."

TYPE A

According to Friedman and Roseman's study, 60 percent of the adult population in this country exhibits Type A behavior. They all share a high propensity for heart attacks, as well as the following characteristics:

Highly competitive

Achievement oriented

Impatient

Fast moving

Time pressured

Emphatic speaking

Type As deal with stress by ignoring it or taking on more of it. Some even consider it a personal challenge: If ten cities in four days was tough, make it twelve! If 60-hour weeks left me weak, make it 80! They seem to go out of their way to pile on more stress. They consistently choose to perform their jobs in the most labor intensive, personally stressful manner possible.

"Stress is for sissies! I can take as much as they can dish out!"

And that seems to be true -- until they get their inevitable wake-up call (see Chapter Five): They have coronaries, their wives leave them, their kids don't know them.

TYPE B

Type Bs constitute everybody else, more or less. Someone with this personality type is often more easygoing and seldom becomes impatient. Type Bs tend to be less involved in the championship image, but are just as serious about their careers as Brother and Sister A. They usually share the following characteristics:

Not motivated by competition alone
Affiliation or power oriented
Patient
Slow moving
Soft spoken

You can tell when a Type A is stressed because his eyes bulge and his face is red and he's screaming and yelling. But with a laid-back Type B, the signals are much more internal.

Type Bs often have a hard time recognizing when they are under stress. They move more slowly and think more deliberately and so stress can actually affect them more severely than it does Type As. They tend to absorb much more of it before it finally hits them. It festers longer and it's more difficult for them to express.

"Oh, this isn't so bad. It doesn't really bother me too much."

Their stomachs start burning, their colons start spasming and their hands start shaking. And then they usually blame themselves.

As you might imagine, each of these personality types profiled in this pioneering research study reacts differently to stress.

A CHAMELEON FOR THE 90S

Whatever your stress type, in the 90s your personal effectiveness will increasingly depend on your ability to produce both types of behavior at will.

In other words, you must become a "Type C."

EXAMPLE. I once worked with a grade school principal who was a Type C. Normally, she was soft-spoken and patient to a fault. She spoke in measured tones and never raised her voice or became excited. She seemed to operate in only one gear; I think it was first.

But when this small, quiet woman needed to, she could shift into overdrive. At appropriate moments (you know, time to kick ass) her gentle, murmuring voice would erupt into staccato shrieks, and anyone standing in her way would suddenly be bisected with tiny footprints.

Her eruptions were all the more effective because she rarely indulged in them. She used a Type A cover to become instantly more effective.

While it may be impossible to change your physiology, it is certainly possible to change your behavior -- for short periods, anyway. If you can learn to change your behavior from A to B and back again as needed -- take on the appropriate, protective coloration -- your chances of succeeding, both at home and at work, will improve dramatically.

You will want to make these situational adaptations for a variety of reasons:

To Reach a Specific Goal

Tell yourself, "If I don't start pumping some high octane enthusiasm, we are not going to make our deadline. I'll gun it until we finish, and then it's back to B-sics."

For a Specific Length of Time

Tell yourself, "For right now, I'll be So-and-so's administrative assistant. I'll be a Type B and I'll walk softly and learn everything I can and then, someday, I'll run this company."

To Adapt To a Superior's Style

Tell yourself, "Okay, this guy is not rewarding butt-kickers. He prefers team players. I'll just lighten up a bit, show him I'm one of the team, then, when he needs someone with some juice, I'll be there."

Whatever your stress type, and whether your daily stress level is high, low, or, as Goldilocks said, "just right," to be effective in the 90s you must develop effective strategies for coping with stress.

And remember: Sometimes, the best strategy is to do nothing at all.

EXERCISE FOR CHAPTER EIGHT

Sixteen Stress Management Strategies
What Will Work For You?

As you read through the suggestions below, try *just one,* as a beginning stress reliever. Try to keep an open mind and use the following criteria for your selection.

● I will do this *now.*
● I will research this more and then try it.
● This is not comfortable for me at this time.

1. Develop a different attitude. ❑
2. Get a checkup. ❑
3. Get adequate rest. ❑
4. Watch your diet. ❑
5. Exercise. ❑
6. Do relaxation exercises. ❑
7. Meditate. ❑
8. Change your reaction patterns. ❑
9. Adapt your environment. ❑
10. Listen to music. ❑
11. Take a break. ❑
12. Express your anger. ❑
13. Take a vacation. ❑
14. Talk it out. ❑
15. Slow down. ❑
16. Do something for others. ❑

Self Management = Stress Management + Time Management

9

TIME:
USE IT OR LOSE IT

Believe it or not, I hear statements like this all the time: "Look, I know I need to manage my time more effectively, but to do that I'd have to be a lot more uptight and compulsive. It's just not worth it."

Here's another one I hear with numbing regularity:

"If I have to watch a clock all the time, all the fun is going to go out of my life!"

And one more:

"Look, I'm a creative person. Time management is for pencil-pushing geeks and dull, anal retentive consultants like you!"

(That last one is a direct quote -- directed at me. Ah, there's nothing like working with open-minded people.)

All of these statements are so wrong. The fact is, no one -- and I mean no one -- can become truly effective without learning to manage our most precious and most limited resource: time. Managing time is such a fundamental skill we should probably add it to The Three Rs and teach it to our children in grammar school.

Anyone who thinks good time managers are neurotic White Rabbits, constantly looking at their watches and then scurrying on to their next "important date" couldn't be more wrong. Good time managers -- even the busiest execs -- have all the time they need for their work, their families and even themselves.

Because good time managers are in control of their lives. They understand that time is a limited resource. They know that, no matter how thin you stretch it, you'll never get more than 24 hours out of a day. And they understand Laekin's Law, one of the most important time management maxims: There's always enough time for the important things.

TIME FOR TRUTHS

This kind of personal effectiveness, this kind of control, is something each of us, if we're really honest with ourselves, want in our lives. If you manage your time as badly as I used to, you probably think good time management is some kind of genetic talent, a trait you've just got to be born with, like green eyes or size 36" hips. But I'm here to tell you, that is simply not true. In fact, I'm convinced that anyone can become an effective time manager.

Even you.

But before you plant your feet and set yourself to take control of your time once and for all, you need to stop and take a moment to get a clear understanding of the role and character of time in western life and culture. You'll need to look at what I call the three *time truths*.

#1. *Time Talks*

Are your ears burning? Well, they should be. That's what happens when you're being talked about (at least that's what my mother used to say). In fact, if there's any truth at all to that old saying, you should look like you've been sleeping with hot coal earmuffs. Because, wherever you go, whatever you do, time is talking about you -- that is, the way you use time.

Are you always late? That says something about you. Are you always early? That says something else. Are you so prompt people say they can set their clocks by you? That says something, too.

Time speaks loudly and in volumes. It tells people an incredible amount about who you are and what's important to you. And people listen, both consciously and unconsciously. They collect observations in their minds, add them to their ever-shifting picture of you, and come quickly and irrevocably to certain conclusions. Conclusions that shift that picture in directions you don't necessarily want it to go.

If you're always late for our appointments, you're telling me I'm not that important to you. That's *my time* you're using -- wasting -- and you're using it to tell me I'm not a priority.

Do you warn me to wait and not start the meeting without you because you're always late? If you do, you're telling me you can't be trusted. You're saying, "Don't worry, I'll disappoint you." You can't even trust yourself. Why on earth should I trust you?

Do you arrive on time, but take forever to get on with the business at hand? That's what a salesperson I worked with used to do. He honestly felt he was ramming his product down his clients' throats if he got right into his pitch, or even told them right off what he was there for. He would start each sales call with a lot of small talk: How're the kids? How's your wife? How was your vacation? These pleasantries usually took five to eight minutes too long -- and made his clients uncomfortable.

After a while, it took him two or three appointments to close the same sale -- if anyone ever asked to see him again.

Another client was always early. He thought that was good. How could it be bad to be a little early? Right? This is a manifestation of an odd quirk I've noticed in the way Americans think: If a little is good (you're on time), a lot would be great (you're early). Actually, by showing up early, my client was telling his clients that he was anxious, that his schedule wasn't full enough. It made him look like an amateur.

It didn't help that he talked fast, launched right into his pitch and then started shoving contracts under people's noses. "These are very busy people I'm calling on," he would tell me. "I think it's rude to waste their time."

Neither of these people understood the difference between "efficient" and "effective" use of their time. The old time/motion studies used to tell us that efficiency was all. I don't believe that's true today, if it ever was. Efficiency means "ready to go;" effective means "ready to go when the moment's right." It's about *process*. You can't, after all, call a meeting and then immediately call for a vote -- as *efficient* as that might be. The time it takes to make everyone comfortable -- the time it *actually* takes -- isn't wasted, either.

As you become more aware of the way you use time, these two concepts will become clearer, and the things time is saying about you will be music to your ears.

#2. *Time Is Relative*
Not only does time talk about you, it speaks in a number of different dialects. That's because time, at different times and places and in different circumstances, means different things to different people.

Have you ever noticed how time drags when you are, say, waiting in line at the grocery store or a ticket office? But doesn't it seem to fly, as they say, when you're having fun? It took seven months to plan the ceremony, but only three seconds to say "I do." But the moment it took to say those two words seemed to last forever. You were pregnant for nine months (Dads go through it, too), but if you're in labor for 30 minutes; 30 minutes seems like 30 years!

The circumstances I'm talking about can be internal as well as external. If you're anxious to get started on your vacation, your last day can drag on. If you're going through a divorce, time seems to be suspended. If you love the task you're engaged in, time is on wings again.

Time is also relative to our age, our health and even our biorhythms. Time is also relative to our expectations and the level of our anxiety. It's even relative to the weather.

What this idea boils down to is that time has *relative value*. A painting contractor I was helping, for example, told me he was having a hard time collecting his invoices from his customers. He said they resented his bill and he couldn't understand why.

As it turned out, he was not telling his customers *from the beginning* how much time a job would take. He didn't do it to be malicious or dishonest; he really didn't know that his customers didn't know. To him, painting a two-story commercial building was a 55-hour job. He knew that almost instinctively after years in the business. But his customers weren't painters, and to many of them, the job simply wasn't worth 55 hours.

Other clients, partners in an ad agency, would spend 25 to 30 hours on a project. They would work on weekends and on through the night.

"We're working so hard," they'd say. "We're solving problems. We're meeting needs."

Sure they were meeting needs -- unfortunately, not their clients'. All it would have taken was a 15-minute phone call they "didn't have time for" to ask their client if they were on the right track. How much do you suppose that call was worth, relatively?

Both the painter and my friends at the ad agency were missing the important distinction between "activity" and "productivity." You have to ask yourself what a good investment of your time would be in a given circumstance. Do we really need to discuss this agenda four more times before we actually do anything? Is a face-to-face meeting really necessary? Or could I give you the information you need over the phone?

You might feel very productive if you make, say, ten sales calls a day. But if you don't book the biz, it's just activity.

#3. *Time Indicates Importance*

People are very conscious of how much time you give them. I often meet managers who like to wander around their company facilities, talking to their employees (a practice I think is very effective for a number of reasons I've already mentioned). It's always very revealing to me to wander around with them. When I do this, I can always tell which employees are doing well, and which ones aren't cutting the mustard. And I can do it without the manager saying a word to me about his workers' performance.

How do I do it? By simply observing how much time he spends with each employee. Some get a wave. Some get a pat on the back and a handshake with a few seconds of eye contact. Some get a, "How's your husband doing?" and a couple of seconds of listening. Others actually get three to five minutes with lots of listening, lots of eye-contact and direct responses to comments and questions.

Look at it this way: If I tell you, "You have an appointment with President Bush and we've budgeted 30 minutes," I'm saying one thing about you. If I tell you, "You've got five minutes to shake the President's hand," I'm saying something else.

So, while time talks about you, you can use it to say a few things to and about others, too. You can drop everything, for example, for an important client (make sure they know you're doing it). You can stop off at your secretary's desk and sit and chat for a while.

You can also risk telling your children they aren't important enough to you to give them any of your time. You can rush your friends in and out or relegate them to quick, say-nothing phone calls.

We all know instinctively how precious and irreplaceable time is. The way you spend your time ration plugs right back into Laekin's Law: "There's always time for the important things."

Everybody knows it.

GETTING A GRIP ON YOUR TIME

What does it take, then, to really get a grip on your time management problems? The question reminds me of the joke that asks, "How many psychiatrists does it take to change a lightbulb?" The answer is: "Only one, but the lightbulb has to be willing to change." So it is when you want to make more effective use of your time; you have to be willing to take the steps that lead to successful time management.

WAKE UP AND SMELL THE COFFEE

Your first step toward better control of your time, (should you be willing to take it) is to find out exactly what you are currently doing with your time. I emphasize the word *exactly*, because this is something you just can't afford to guess at. You probably know someone who never balances his checkbook. He's always guessing whether or not he's got enough to cover this or that bill with a check. It just doesn't work, does it? He may get by with it for awhile, but, oh yeah, he forgot to include that check at the cleaners, and, dang! there was that check for the kids' jeans. Pretty soon the checks start coming back because he let his money slip through the cracks.

You can't afford to do that. You need to know -- really know -- where your time is going.

So, just as you record where, when and how much money you spend in a check register, you need to record where, when and how you spend your time in a time log.

In designing your time log, you don't need to record every single, waking second of every, single day. If you're an office administrator, you may want to jot down what you are doing every 15 minutes. If you are a real estate developer (a business where things happen about every six months), you really only have to document weekly increments.

But most of us need to look at what we're doing about every half hour.

Wait! Don't shout! I can hear your objections just fine. I'll summarize them, if I may, with this paraphrase: "I can't possibly do this. I don't have time. How am I going to get any work done if I have to stop everything to fill out a form every half hour? This is going to take more time than it's worth!"

Don't worry, I can almost guarantee you are currently wasting far more time than you will spend with your time log. In fact, I can guarantee you are going to be astonished!

A LIST, A LIST, MY KINGDOM FOR A LIST

For most people, two weeks of carefully recording your activities should be enough to get an idea of where your time is being spent. You will probably be making better use of your time before the end of that period, though. You won't be able to help it, once you start seeing how much time you are wasting.

The next thing you should do is get into the habit of making lists. I'm a firm believer in the power of the list. Use it for a while and you will be, too.

What, exactly, do you put on your list? As you can imagine, simply writing down the things you have to do each day on a note card isn't going to do much for your effectiveness until you begin to make some decisions about the relative importance of the things you write down.

So you have to set priorities. The simplest way to do that is to designate the items on your "To Do" list as "A," "B" or "C" items. Your "A" category should include tasks that are both urgent *and* important. "B" items should be those tasks that are *either* urgent *or* important. "C" items should be the ongoing chores that should get done sooner or later, but could suffer some delay.

As you sit down to prioritize the items on your list, you should also be aware of certain Time Traps into which people commonly fall.

TIME TRAPS

The first Time Trap most people with time management problems seem to fall into is simple failure to heed Brigid's Law, which goes like this: *Everything takes longer than you think it will.*

If you get nothing else from this book but a firm, unshakeable belief in Brigid's Law, you will have gotten your money's worth a thousand times over.

Why is it so many people never stop to determine how long a task will really take to complete? Oh, people throw out numbers like, "ten minutes, at most," like they've just jotted down the height and width of the thing and rolled up their tape measures.

Everything takes longer than you think it will -- and everything should.

Another Time Trap you need to take care to avoid is the tendency to designate all of the items on your list As and Bs. I see examples of this Trap quite often when I'm consulting with people who are new to management. Their hearts pound and their palms sweat because everything is vitally important. And then someone comes in and gives them something else that must be done right now and they fall apart.

But that's silly! You can't accomplish everything *right now*. You may not have enough information to complete the task. Or you may need to involve others who are not available right now. Or it may be something that will require a long term effort or a lot of thought.

And everything takes longer than you think it will, anyway.

And here, *here* is one of the most dangerous elements of this particular Time Trap. If every item on your list is an A or a B, when are you going to have time to stop to think?

A recent study of some top American business executives revealed that 80 percent of those surveyed failed to schedule any time for thinking. I find this statistic frightening! If you never make time to think, you only act. You fail to see the relative importance of the task you're doing. You're just blasting away with a shotgun, hoping it'll hit something.

The truly effective people I work with are sharpshooters with deadly aim. Truly effective people budget the time they need to think things over. They never act unconsciously.

People who fall into this trap have failed to ask themselves this all-important question: "What is the best use of my time right now?" The answer may be, "The best use of my time right now is to step back and take a good look at what we're doing here." It may be, "Do nothing."

Of course you may already be suffering from a version of this Time Trap through no action of your own. You may have the kind of job in which you have to respond to an immediate superior's constantly changing priorities. If you are a secretary, for example, you may have to do whatever your boss tells you to do, without negotiation.

There are three things you can do if you are in the kind of a work environment in which someone is always changing your priorities: 1) accept, 2) change or 3) leave. I know secretaries who have lived with this kind of situation until they were tearing their hair out, who then went to their bosses, explained the problem and found them very understanding and responsive. But I'm afraid that's not the norm.

One executive secretary I've worked with says, "When I go into work, I try never to have any expectations of being in control of my workday. I have nothing planned. The boss comes in and whatever his priorities are, I just adapt to them. That's my job."

Is there really any wonder that the occupational category with the most stress is "secretary?"

This brings me to one of the most subtle Time Traps of all. A lot of people think they only need time management skills for their careers. But you must remember: Personally effective people use their time management skills to schedule time for all the activities of their lives.

Are all the As on your list job-oriented? What about scheduling some time to be with your family during the holidays? Isn't that an A?

Remember: My definition of an A item includes those tasks that are both urgent and important. Another way to look at that is to think of an A item as one which requires much needed results. Those results for your career should center around money, but the dollar is not the coin of all realms.

There's a huge opportunity cost associated with a "work, work, work" plan for budgeting your time. People who fail to schedule time for their children's school activities or regular trips to the gym, find out, sooner or later, that their lives are leaking away.

In other words, you can't be truly effective if you're burning out. Effective time management is about making smart choices. It's also about knowing that, *hey, I deserve to survive.*

THE BALANCING ACT OF THE 90s

Personally effective people deserve and demand to be fully realized human beings. They are wonderful, interesting and productive people because of it. They take a wider view of their lives than those who just look to their jobs for fulfillment. As you begin to take on your time management problems, take a tip from these people and pay attention to these seven areas in which personally effective people focus their time management efforts:

Career Satisfaction

Not just your paycheck. Ask yourself if you are giving yourself enough time to do the kind of job you want to do.

Learning And Education

Especially education outside your comfort zone. One of the reasons some people find time management such a problem, such a black hole, is that their focus is so narrow that they become bored. But sign these people up for a Tai Chi class and they begin to think about Eastern religions and fluidity of movement (or whatever). And they find that parts of their brains are being stimulated that would not be in another industry seminar. Time spent learning about something *other* than work is time that will pay off in more effective performance on the job.

Personal Relationships

Not just your family, but friends. *People who can't help your career at all.*

Leisure Satisfaction

This includes not only exercise, but hobbies and other interests you want to develop. The biggest challenge we will ever face in our lifetimes in my opinion is retirement. We're all going to have a lot of time on our hands someday. Make sure you schedule time now to develop a part of your life to live for when you pick up your last paycheck.

Status And Respect

This is a critical and surprisingly, a frequently ignored area. Are you making time to do things that will help you to become known and respected in your field? Your church? Your community? You are more than what you do at the office. Make time to show your stuff.

Spiritual Growth
This category includes anything that brings you peace of mind. It could be your religion or any number of things that fill in the gaps.

Other
Okay, "other" looks kind of silly, but there are other things out there -- like your passion for helping the homeless or coaching Little League -- that don't easily fit into any of the above categories. But you've got to make time for this other stuff to have a full and effective life.

THE PLAN'S THE THING
After you've spent a couple of weeks faithfully recording your activities in your favorite time management log, you'll have a pretty good idea of exactly how you spend your time. Your next step on the road to effective time management is to ask yourself four questions:

What Are Some Time Wasters I Encounter At Work Or At Home?
EXAMPLE. Every time I try to get a map out of the glove compartment of my car, an incredible cache of junk explodes into my front seat and I spend ten frustrating minutes searching for the map and then stuffing everything back in.
EXAMPLE. Part of my job is to make copies for everyone in the office, and I have to make about 20 trips a day to the copier. But the copy machine is

169

located at the opposite end of the building from my desk.

What Are Some Ways I Waste Other People's Time?

EXAMPLE. I committed to this telephone appointment, then the first words out of my mouth are, "I'm not ready!"

EXAMPLE. I send everything by express mail. People find this very irritating because it communicates a sense of urgency that's often not real. It's like a constant shock and they eventually resent it.

What Are Some Ways I Could Work More Effectively?

EXAMPLE. I'm looking for a job and I've got to get my resume together, but I spend three days working on cover letters.

Again, I'm not talking about merely doing something faster. (If you're doing the wrong thing, who cares how fast you get it done?) You must prioritize correctly, which means, of course, that you must make the right choices. That usually means doing the hardest job first. Though I need to work on both my resume and my cover letter, I can't send the letters without the resume.

What Are Some Ways I Can Help My Supervisors, Co-Workers and Family Members To Be More Effective?

EXAMPLE. The number one complaint from working parents is that getting children ready in the morning -- getting dressed, eating breakfast, getting off to school -- is a nightmare.

THE STRATEGIES

Ask yourself the prior questions often throughout your life and you will make dramatic and continual improvements in your management of time. But, don't immobilize yourself with "analysis paralysis." Eventually you've got to take action. Invest some time in the following strategies and they'll yield time dividends you can take to the bank.

#1. *Do Your Homework.*

Putting your goals in writing starts the *forced-choice process*. The essence of time management is a series of choices. When you take the idea of what you want to accomplish and you put it down in black and white, you create a yardstick against which you can measure your progress.

A good example of this is a salesperson I met recently who had just finished a grueling, two-year sales course.

"Wow," I said when she told me of her accomplishment, "that's great. What do you hope to do with it?"

"Well," she said, "I hope to teach and consult."

Teach and consult? Without an MBA? Not in this life! The course she took was good, tough and it could make her the greatest salesperson in the world, but her goal was to teach and consult. For that you need the certification that comes with a traditional degree. Had she done her homework and put her goals in writing, it would have been obvious to everyone in her life that the course she was working so hard on *would not* help her achieve those goals.

#2.   *Focus On Objectives, Not Activities.*

This is the difference between being busy and getting things done. An objective is a piece of your goal. Or, more precisely, it's an incremental step toward your goal. (For instance, I bought my walking shoes, so now I'm that much closer to my exercise program.) Make sure your activity really is moving you toward your goal. You don't just go out one morning and pick up a four-year degree. You have to register, show up, study, keep at it.

Shopping, while you may need to do it, won't get you closer to that degree. Don't fool yourself into thinking your busy day at the mall was a productive one.

#3.   *Set At Least One Important Objective Daily and Achieve It.*

Goals are really ahead of you -- a year or more down the road. Objectives, however, can be accomplished daily. What am I doing today to get a better job? What am I doing today to become a better parent? What am I doing today to lose weight?

It's important to do something every day because that's how life is lived. Some of us, if we could, would go through a week at a time and get things over with. But our lives are lived *day by day*. That's how your goals will be achieved.

Also, when you set daily objectives you can actually achieve, you have those little successes along the way toward your goal that keep you going. It's not enough to say, "Someday I'm going to get there."

#4. *Question All Of Your Activities.*

The reason many people don't have good time management skills is because the whole process is a series of tough choices. If you have set your long-term goals down in writing and you are achieving daily objectives toward that goal, there will be some things you can no longer do. You have to be able to say, "I'm sorry, I can't take part in that anymore, even though I enjoyed it at the time."

It's like dieting. I want to be thin more than I want that piece of cake. If you want to have more time, more control over your time, more quality time, you are going to have to let this or that go.

And you have to recognize that those choices are coming. Question your activities. Constantly say, "This is what I want, but this is what I'm doing. I guess that doesn't make sense anymore."

#5. *Get Rid Of At Least One Time Waster From Your Life Each Month.*

It's a fact of human psychology that it takes adults about 28 days to change a behavior. We need lots of repetition, folks, so don't try to become Super Time Manager overnight. Just pick one time waster -- say, one hour of TV each night -- and work at cutting it out of your life. You will need to go about a month without those TV shows to know that you've really kicked the habit.

Time wasting isn't all bad. In fact, what you might decide to do, once you get control of your time, is to waste *more* of it. The idea is to make choices about your time and not be the victim of bad habits.

173

#6. *Make A To-Do List Every Day.*

When I'm speaking before a group, I will sometimes stop and ask everybody in the audience who is making a mental grocery list, or planning what they are going to do when we're finished for the day to raise their hands. Usually, about half the room responds. Then I tell them to turn their notes over, write down whatever they were thinking about and then we get on with it. This doesn't usually offend anyone, because it makes the point that most of us habitually clutter our minds with a thousand things, wasting our mental energy trying to remember them.

That's why you should make a to-do list every day. Write your plans down. That way you won't clutter your mind. You won't be distracted by trivia you don't need to think about. And your plans will become real and visible.

In fact, I recommend two to-do lists: one for work, one for home. If you don't keep both, your personal life will inevitably be sacrificed. That's not going to make you more effective -- and it's no way to live.

#7. *Schedule Your Time Every Day To Make Sure You Accomplish The Most Important Things First, But Leave Room For The Unexpected -- Including Interruptions.*

Time management expert Alex McKenzie recommends scheduling no more than 50 percent of your time. I believe this is the only truly effective way to schedule your time. Even hardcore salespeople don't sell every hour of every day. If a salesperson schedules sales calls back-to-back throughout the day, he's going to need at least a day to write them up, service them, etc.

174

Don't think for a minute this approach will leave you with a lazy day with half as much work to do. You'll still be as busy as you ever were, but you might not feel so harassed and harried. You'll have room to make adjustments. You'll be more effective.

#8. *Make Sure The First Hour Of Your Workday Is Productive.*

Some people really question this statement. They say, "Hey, I'm an afternoon person." Well, if your real workday starts an hour after lunch, fine. But give yourself the gift of making one solid hour productive at the start.

This strategy works because, well, there's something about feeling ahead of the game that makes us more productive overall. If you feel like you are eating dust in last place, your productivity level will certainly reflect this.

In fact, many companies start each day with a quiet hour of protected time. No meetings. No calls. No distractions. Employees of those companies report that hour is often the most productive 60 minutes of their day -- often yielding three hours worth of work.

#9. *Set Time Limits For Every Task You Undertake.*

There are two reasons to set time limits. The first is to keep from being bogged down in tasks you are not equipped to perform. Maybe you don't have enough information, maybe you're not the right person for the job. Whatever the reason, setting time limits allows you to set a task aside before it engulfs you.

The second reason for setting time limits is to teach you just how much time various tasks and activities take. Most people don't really know how long things take. Think of *The Rule of the Dirty Car:* Your car is finally so dirty, you just can't stand it so you say, "I'll just take 10 minutes and get it out of the way." But once you cover the filthy beast in soapy water you find that it's *really* dirty. The more you smear it around, the worse it gets.

Then you finally get it rinsed off, and you just can't seem to get it dry. Then you notice the interior is a mess. Then you notice the waterspots. Now you've spent a frantic hour splotching up your dirty car.

Don't do this to yourself! *Everything takes longer than you think it will.* If you are going to go pick up the children from school, it's going to take 20 minutes even though the school is only three minutes away.

We need to find out just how much time is required for the tasks and activities in our lives, otherwise we erode our trust in our own abilities. But don't worry, it gets easier and easier.

#10. *Take The Time and Make The Effort To Do Things The Right Way The First Time.*

One of the biggest consumer issues of the 90s is quality. In management, that translates into *quality control.* Taking the time to do things right the first time gives you quality control over your life. It gives you confidence in yourself. You don't waste your time going back to do it over later. Make sure you have everything you need to do it right the first time; all the information, tools and personnel. If you don't, you still have this thing on your list that hasn't been done (though you spent the time doing it once already). This thing will grow, as it intrudes on the time you've allocated for other activities, until it becomes a kind of virus, infecting your entire day.

Don't do this to yourself! *Measure twice; cut once.*

#11. *Plan At Least One Hour Each Day Of Uninterrupted Time For Your Most Important Chores.*

You've got to make sure you have this protected time worked into your schedule every day if you ever want to get control of your time. The average person gets interrupted 60 times a day in a business setting. It's impossible to stay on track with that level of interruptions. A lot of people call in sick and do their work at home. But that's silly. You should be able to work at work. And you can, if you create the environment for it.

#12. *Get Into The Habit Of Finishing What You Start.*

Someone said to me the other day, "I always do three things at once, and I never finish any of them." Now that's what I call effective! I asked her how it made her feel, and she said, "Lousy!" No kidding.

Time management means: Beginning, Middle and *End.* Finishing what you start is a key habit of personally effective people. It has a lot to do with learning to say "no."

"Sorry, Ed, I can't get involved in that right now, I've got to finish this project." It's the way to get things done.

And since people learn so much more about us from our behavior than they do from our advice, finishing what you start is a powerful tool for a supervisor or a parent. It gives you lots of credibility.

Most important, it gives you credibility with yourself. Loose ends sound like light, fluttery tassels in the wind. But they're really heavy baggage.

#13. Conquer Procrastination.

When we put something off, it's either because we don't want to do it, or we don't know how to do it. I don't think, in and of itself, procrastination is such a big problem. If you follow the other guidelines in this list of strategies, how can you procrastinate?

Answer: You can't.

All these strategies are really just good habits. As we assimilate these habits and become more effective, we begin to make better and better choices -- better choices about how to use our time. In the face of strong and effective time management habits, procrastination evaporates.

#14. Don't Spend Time On Less Important Things When You Could Be Spending It On More Important Ones.

Remember: There's always time for the important things. Take a look at what you are actually making time for. The way you are living may reveal that it is, in fact, really important for you to watch a lot of TV right now. What does that say about you? What are you going to do about it?

It's exhausting to me to be around people who always complain that they don't have time for the things they really want to do. It's obvious to everybody but them that what's important to them is what they *are* doing. Their actions are saying, "I'm not paying any attention to my children because it's more important to me to fold the laundry and get it into the drawers than it is to talk to them." Actions always speak louder than words.

#15. *Take Time For Yourself: Time To Relax, Time To Live, Time To Dream.*
Personally effective people are not workaholic machines. They are well-rounded, interesting human beings with lots of energy and enthusiasm for their lives and the people in them. They are effective time managers so they automatically have time to relax, live and dream.

The reason most people begin to recognize that they have time management problems is because they have none of these in their lives. But that's no way to live and you know it (or you wouldn't have read this chapter).

Here's where I'll make you a promise: If you incorporate any of the above strategies into your life -- make a list, eliminate a time waster, do things right the first time -- you will be well on your way to improving the quality of your life.

This is the payoff: Enjoy!

EXERCISE FOR CHAPTER NINE

Now Why Didn't I Think Of That?

As you take control of your time and your life, you need to get a handle on your own obstacles. Complete the exercise below, either alone, with co-workers or spouse to find out where your precious time is going.

Time Wasters I Encounter at Work and Methods to Overcome Them:
1.
2.
3.
4.

Ways I Waste Other People's Time and Ways to Stop:
1.
2.
3.
4.

Four Ways I Could Do My Work More Effectively:
1.
2.
3.
4.

Four Ways I Could Help My Supervisor Be More Effective:
1.
2.
3.
4.

CHAPTER **10**

EVERYDAY LEADERSHIP SKILLS

When I first met Greg a few years ago, he was working as a sales rep for a medium-sized television station in Northern California. He was an extremely hard working, highly motivated, genuinely stand-out performer. So, though he hadn't been with the station as long as many of the other salespeople working there, I wasn't surprised when he told me he was applying for the company's recently-vacated sales manager position. And I had little doubt he could handle the job.

Unfortunately, the station's management did not share my opinion of Greg's abilities and he was passed over. The company filled the sales manager spot with a good old boy whose management style fit snugly somewhere between Scarlet O'Hara ("I'll think about that tomorrow") and Richard Nixon ("I am not a crook").

He lasted about four months, and the mess he left behind was daunting to say the least.

Except to Greg. He thrived on this kind of challenge and when he landed the promotion the second time around, he went immediately to work building an effective sales team. Unlike his predecessor, he carefully communicated his goals to his people. He gave them the support they needed. And he administered the consequences of failure to

181

reach the team's goals. All of which led to an unsettling increase in the sales department's turnover rate.

But Greg was relentless. For months he stuck to his plan. He had formulated a clear picture of what the sales department should look like "fixed," and, instead of hiring more salespeople who were not up to the job he had in mind, he brought in only those people who fit his vision.

As you might guess, Greg's first quarter was an inferno. His second quarter cooled a bit, but the heat was on for his first eight months on the job. During that time, Greg experienced the beginnings of an ulcer, his personal credibility was called into question and he made a lot of enemies.

But by the end of those eight months he had turned the entire department around. He had surrounded himself with people who knew what he wanted them to do, were able to do it and, more important, were *willing* to do it. As the station's sales figures improved, so did Greg's credibility, his health and his paycheck. He had done what needed to be done. He became something that is about as rare as hens' teeth: an effective leader.

LEAD, FOLLOW OR GET OUT OF THE WAY

If there is a single end to the pursuit of personal effectiveness (and I'm not sure there is), I believe it is leadership.

"Leadership?" I hear you say. "Who needs to be a leader? I sure don't! I mean, I want to be personally effective and all that, but hey, I don't want to run for Governor or claw my way into the CEO's chair at a Fortune 500 company. Frankly, I don't even want to be the sales manager of this place. Why should I give a hoot about developing my leadership skills?"

Well, Kemosabi, one reason you should care about such things is that we no longer live in a world where one can survive as the Lone Ranger. With the proliferation of television, telephones and computers, our evolving world economy, and freedom breaking out all over Eastern Europe and the Soviet Union, individuals, communities and even nations are becoming more *interdependent* everyday.

Even if you're not interested in public office, top management or international trade, you probably live in a neighborhood, attend a church and/or care for a family. So, sometime, somewhere, unless you hunt for your own meat with flint-tipped arrows and go it solo in a cave in the Rockies, you are going to need to enlist the cooperation of others. (After all, even the Masked Man had to work with Tonto once in a while.)

And that takes *leadership*. Not necessarily captain-of-the-ship leadership, but the everyday leadership skills I'm going to talk about in this chapter.

COMPONENTS OF LEADERSHIP

Let's start with a definition of leadership. The best one I know can be found in Drea and Patricia Zigarmi and Ken Blanchard's wonderful book on situational leadership, *Leadership and the One Minute Manager*. They define leadership as, "The process of influencing the activities of an individual or group toward a goal or accomplishment." I like this definition so much because it emphasizes a crucial fact about leadership that you must understand to become an effective leader: If you can't take people with you, you aren't going anywhere.

Horse Power

To fully understand the dynamics of everyday leadership, you will need another definition. As you proceed in your efforts to influence groups and individuals it is essential that you understand the meaning of *power*.

Oooh! I can almost feel you shudder at the very mention of the word. And I can almost see the pictures of Adolf Hitler, Julius Caesar and Ghengis Khan dancing before your eyes.

"I can sure see what you mean about not playing the Lone Ranger in today's society," might be your comment about now. "But this is too much! Now you want me to conquer the world!"

Hold your horses, Kemosabi! When we talk about "power" in the context of personal effectiveness, we're talking about "influence." Influence is the ability to affect someone's character, beliefs or actions. If you can do any of those things, you've got power.

Power is an incredibly misunderstood word. We forget sometimes that the ability to influence people and events can be an extremely positive force. And the fact is, effective leadership has a lot to do with doing just that.

In their exploration of power, Zigarmi and Blanchard clarify their use of the word with seven "power bases" which I have found to be edifying:

#1. Coercive Power

This is the one you are probably choking on. It's the type of power I see most often used in business. It's based on fear. The leader who uses "coercive power" induces compliance with a threat of punishment. "Do it or you're fired," is a phrase that sums up this type of power base pretty well.

We all know about the negative uses of coercive power, but sometimes coercive power can be used as a positive tool. Depending on with whom you are working, it can be just the right thing to do. And without it in your arsenal, you may find yourself unarmed as a leader.

EXAMPLE. Millie was an elementary school principal who recently found herself in a new school, saddled with a janitor who for years had been getting away with what can only be described as murder. Millie tried every trick she had ever used in managing difficult teachers, treating him as she would have wanted to be treated, as a professional and an equal.

But the janitor refused to respond. His back was always hurt; he never seemed to understand exactly what she wanted him to do: "You want me to do what? I've never had to do that before."

"My back was against the wall," Millie said. "I had to threaten to write him up and document every bit of work he left undone. I had to threaten to see him fired. Threats! The only thing this guy would respond to were threats!"

"Not threats," I told her, "consequences." By accepting that coercion was the only type of leadership Millie's janitor would follow, she was able to influence him to do the maintenance job that her school needed done. She was able to do her job and establish herself as an effective leader.

#2. *Connective Power*

This type of power is based on the leader's real or perceived access to influential individuals or groups. One reason people join service organizations, such as the United Way or Rotary Club (besides, of course, a genuine interest in helping others) is that such memberships often lead to "connective power."

One of the more positive aspects of the highly mobile nature of modern society is that it has resulted in relatively open access to these kinds of groups. Though there are "old boys" clubs, and there are a few, inaccessible "in" groups, you don't have to be born with connections nowadays. You can develop your own fairly easily.

In fact, sometimes you actually have greater connective power as an outsider. I've found that to be true in my own business. As an outside consultant, I often have access to the very top executives in a company. Though I work for them for a time, it is in the role of vendor. I'm never really part of the team, and so, do not share in any of the political in-fighting or dysfunctional roles that often exist (the reasons I'm there in the first place). I demonstrate my effectiveness, and then I'm outta there!

The groups or individuals which are the source of your connective power do not necessarily have to be influential in and of themselves. Moms and Dads, for example, band together in PTAs and wind up with tremendous connective power. Almost any kind of shared experience creates a connection that yields influence because of what you have in common.

#3. *Expert Power*

Are you a doctor? A lawyer? Do you have some kind of expertise, say, with computers? If you do, then you have "expert power." A lot of secretaries have expert power because they know everything the boss knows -- and, frankly, sometimes more. Even lacking any other expertise, a secretary is an expert *on the boss.* And that gives that secretary a lot of power.

"Well, gee, he said he didn't want to be disturbed, but I'm sure he'd want to make an exception for you, Bob."

Or: "I'm inputting that information right now, Bob, but it's not ready. Maybe you ought to call back later."

Get it? But easily the clearest example of expert power is any individual with a diploma, license or other certification hanging on his wall. Those pieces of paper have a lot of *power* in them because they constitute objective, verifiable evidence of that individual's expertise. They "prove" that he is an expert.

Such physical evidence is vital. In order for expert power to work, you have to be known as an expert. In addition to displays of diplomas and licenses, you must wrap yourself in the trappings of your expertise. A doctor wears her white lab coat and stethoscope; a repairman carries his toolbox.

There's a strong placebo effect associated with this type of power. After all, a physician has only to walk into the room wearing her white coat and many people begin to feel better. I always have a tremendous sense of security when I walk into the office of a lawyer or CPA I've hired and I see all the degrees framed and hanging on the walls. They seem to say, "Hey, don't worry. Everything is going to be fine. I'm an expert."

Evidence of expertise creates a wonderful power base and I'm surprised at how many people I meet who voluntarily dilute their expert power, and thus, their effectiveness, with phrases like, "Oh, gee. That's really just an honorary degree. Heck, everybody goes to college!"

Don't do it! It's like throwing out half your ammo, just to be fair to the enemy.

#4. *Referent Power*

If you have "referent power," what you really have is *charisma*. It's the power of personality and the best example of this type of power I can think of is Chrysler president Lee Iaccoca. He splashes his face across billboards and bookshelves, newspapers and magazines, and he smiles at us from our television sets and says, "Love me, love my company."

For Iaccoca, it works; but it may not work forever. This type of power is the most transitory and the least reliable.

Many people in new leadership roles feel they must exude charisma, that if they are quiet or shy they won't be effective leaders.

So, they end up trying to base their leadership solely on their personalities.

This is a very bad move. It leaves these leaders extremely vulnerable. Referent power doesn't work well, for example, on apathetic people, negative people, or to that person who is the opposite of that leader's personality type ("rah-rah" vs. slow and deliberate).

EXAMPLE. When Henry was promoted to vice president of administration he had very little administrative experience -- none, in fact. His background was marketing, and he was good at it. So, as most of us would, when he came up against his deficiencies, he fell back on what he knew.

But his attempts to lead his people with slogans and "rah-rah" failed because, after his we-can-do-it speech, and after his let's-all-pull-together speech, they asked the obvious question: "Pull together to do what?" Henry had no answer to that question. He was removed precipitously and nobody was surprised but him.

If referent power is the only type of power you have going for you, you won't be powerful for long.

#5. *Information Power*

This type of power base may seem at first to be the same as expert power. But it is different in at least one significant way: "Information power" is based on a leader's access to the *latest* information.

EXAMPLE. I know an older, retired businessman whose power and influence in his community is based largely on information power. Though he no longer takes an active part in running his business, he spends about 80-plus percent of his time on the telephone every day.

What's he doing? Listening to gossip. Getting information. Trading it.

Networking. Negotiating. Creating deals. *Brokering power.* He is the person you go to in that community to say, "I need to raise $100,000. Who's got it?" He knows, and he'll tell you. He's an important listening post and he readily shares what he knows. He never stands in the spotlight, but he manipulates the whole show from backstage.

Peter Drucker, in his book, *The New Revolution*, observes that we are truly living in the information age. But it's not just technical information he's talking about. It's information about what the information *means*. In this information age, there's power in understanding what you know and communicating it well.

#6. *Legitimate Power*
What's the difference between a marketing coordinator and a marketing manager? About $10,000 a year. That's an example of the effect of "legitimate power," power that is based on position or title.

If you don't think those two things matter in our society, just count the number of people in this country who stayed up to watch the marriage of Prince Charles and Princess Di (not to mention the throngs of people who buy the *National Enquirer* every week just to read about the latest exploits of "the royals").

Titles are very important in this country. "Executive assistant," "managing editor," "the boss," "the coach," "the owner."

EXAMPLE. Blanche had worked as an executive secretary at several Bay Area companies for many years. She was competent and experienced, but her career was stalled. She seemed to be trapped in a secretarial ghetto.

Then she left her current secretarial position and accepted a job at another firm. The job was nearly the same in every way as the job she had done for so many years -- except that her title at the new company was "administrative assistant," and her salary was larger.

The change inspired her to upgrade her wardrobe, improve her vocabulary and her attendance. Every aspect of her personal effectiveness improved because of the change in title. And it put her on a totally different career path.

Be conscious of your title. (Everybody at the bank is a vice president these days.) It's the way the game is played. Your title can make a tremendous difference in your level of legitimate power.

#7. *Reward Power*
Never underestimate the effectiveness of "reward power." It is, simply put, based on your ability to provide a reward.

The forms of effective rewards are more varied than you might imagine. Such rewards as pay raises and promotions are probably the first to come to mind. But as we enter the 90s, one of the most effective rewards you can offer is *recognition*.

Why? Because there's never enough money. No matter what we make, we always need more. So cash rewards have only a temporary, tenuous hold on us. A new title or position often carries new responsibilities as well as privileges, so we tend to perceive them as rewards for only a short time. Soon, we recognize the trade-offs and the reward loses its effectiveness.

Studies show that what people really care about is something quite different. What we remember after 25 years with a company isn't that we got this raise or that promotion. It isn't that we retired on a pension of $2,000 a month. What we remember is how, over the years, our supervisor recognized our work.

"Yeah, I was Newcomer of the Year, and made the Top Ten Club eight years running. The Old Man himself gave me that plaque."

Those are the kinds of rewards that last; those *feelings* last. A check today is worth nothing tomorrow, but a pat on the back lasts 20 years and is recalled with as much vividness as if it had happened the day before.

The really good news is that just about anybody can give this kind of reward. So you don't have to be Donald Trump to develop this power base. All you need is careful listening skills and a good word.

Building A Strong Power Base

To be an effective leader, you must be in command of at least three of these power bases. Any combination will do it. If you've got, say, information, expertise and the ability to give a reward, it's very likely that you'll be an effective leader. But, though you might have tremendous expertise and the latest information, if you can't pat your followers on the back, you will not be an effective leader. With only two of these power bases you are in a very shaky position.

If you have only one, you are in an incredibly *predictable* and *vulnerable* position. If all you have is, say, coercive power, after a while, your followers will notice that they aren't dead and they aren't scared anymore. ("If she fires me, so what? I was going to quit anyway.") Your single power base evaporates and it's "Bye-bye, Kemosabi!"

FORM FOLLOWS FUNCTION

In their efforts to try to influence the character, beliefs and actions of others, effective leaders employ a number of leadership styles based on the needs of their followers. To be an effective leader, you must be ready to adapt your style to what each leadership situation requires.

Spell It Out

This is the most direct approach and it's often a good place to start. The leader simply tells his followers clearly what it is he wants them to do. While this leadership style may be the most direct, in many ways, it's far from the simplest.

EXAMPLE. Dale was a newly hired sales rep for an auto manufacturer. He went through the company's three-day orientation program and then reported to his manager.

At this point, Dale knew practically nothing about the job he would actually do. He had received only general information during the orientation and he had many basic questions. "Where's my territory?" "Who are my contacts?" "When is the best time to call on them?" "What's my quota?" "How often should I check in with you?"

Dale's manager's job was to answer those questions -- accurately. His ability to communicate accurate information at that point would determine how willing Dale would be to follow him in the future.

So he gave careful and specific directions, easing Dale's fears by showing him he was in capable hands. The manager didn't guess -- *ever*. He spoke from personal experience and prepared Dale for his task using a very "hands-on" leadership style. He took pains to make certain he had done everything he possibly could to give Dale every chance to succeed.

Cheer Them On

This is the next level and it's for followers who have a high level of competence, but a low level of confidence -- like Dale, once he'd finished his orientation program. His supervisor then conducted a productive and informative meeting with Dale and sent him out in the field for a week.

Dale came back to his supervisor and said, "I know all the facts about this job. I know what I'm supposed to do, what you want and how to achieve those results, but I'm ... well, to tell you the truth, I'm a little afraid I don't have what it takes after all."

Dale's manager just smiled and shifted gears. His role now was something more akin to that of a coach than anything else.

"Hey, Dale," the manager said, "everybody gets scared in this racket. But I know the results you've produced elsewhere and I am positive you can handle this. I'm here to help if you need it. Now, what do you need me to do so you can do what you need to do?"

"How about going with me on a few calls?"

"Sure! No sweat."

Dale's manager became his coach, and this coaching was backed up with real support. And he was very effective because, rather than assume he needed more training, or better sales materials, he asked Dale, specifically, what kind of support he needed to get the job done.

Tune Them Up

Once Dale's manager had helped to jump-start his engine, he rolled along pretty well. But he still needed an occasional tune-up.

So his manager obliged by shifting his leadership gears again. His new approach was to use a style that involved periodic problem-solving sessions and role-playing exercises. The manager left Dale alone until he came to him for help with some specific problems.

"You've been there," Dale said. "Based on your experience how do you think I ought to handle it?"

"Okay," the manager said. "So now you've hit this kind of sales resistance. No sweat. First let's try..."

Dale's manager recognizes that there's no need to spell everything out or wave his pompoms. He could see that Dale needed him to act as *mentor*. Recognizing this made his use of this leadership style very effective.

Check Up

This leadership style is for those followers who need little direction or coaching. The leader has delegated tasks to his confident, competent followers and all is well. Except that his followers still need to have their efforts *recognized* to be willing to continue under their leader's influence.

Dale, for example, was doing very well by now. He and his manager had worked most of the bugs out of his sales presentation and he was accomplishing the goals they had agreed upon. Dale didn't really need much of his manager's input any more. He knew his job and he was doing it well.

But Dale's manager was smart. He knew better than to send one of his followers off into the wilderness with no life-line back to camp.

So, the manager shifted again and adapted to his follower's *new* needs. As regularly as possible, he checked in with Dale. He called him into his office and asked him how he was doing, inquired about problems and offered his support. And he did the most important thing he could do for a follower as ready, willing and able as Dale: He patted him on the back.

As I pointed out in the section on referent power, this kind of personal recognition is not only useful, in the 90s *it will be vital.* Dale's manager had led him well up to now. If he had failed to adapt his leadership style to Dale's changing needs, all his efforts would have yielded a disappointed follower who would actually *resist* his leadership later on.

Well, Kemosabi, if you stuck it out this far, and you're not "definitioned" to death, you're probably ready to start applying everything you know about leadership.

But first, to Zigarmi and Blanchard's excellent definition of leadership, I would like to add an observation from my own experience: A big part of the leadership process involves helping people feel the way *they* want to feel about themselves. Far from a simplistic, "they want to feel good about themselves," we must help to create a working environment where taking the risk to get enthused is supported. In many instances, I've been involved with companies that want to reawaken or redirect the energy of the employees. The company spokesperson tells me, "Brigid, we want you to come in and get them all going in the same direction. We want them to care about the customers and to provide excellent customer service." My first question is, "What are you willing to do for *them?*" After a stunned silence, I generally hear, "You mean beyond the bimonthly paycheck?" Pay alone -- without an energizing, challenging work environment -- will not produce the desired results. No amount of pay in the world can substitute for a feeling of pride in the accomplishment of work well done -- and appreciated.

To do this, we must carefully develop and then combine the three essential elements of effective leadership: a clear goal, a clear message and a clear understanding of the needs of our followers.

Keep Your Eye On The Ball
Let's face it: We can't lead anyone anywhere until we know where we're going. Dale's manager, for example, would have had little success leading his new sales rep toward his sales quota if he had had some fuzzy notion about his *goal*. "I want him to be a good salesperson," is not a clear enough goal; it's too general, too vague. "I want him to sell X, by such-and-such," is a specific, definable, *unambiguous* end. Both Dale and his manager would know when he had achieved it.

It's not always enough to clearly see our goals. We must also recognize, in equally unambiguous terms, *the means required to reach our ends.*

Sounds like simple common sense, you say? Maybe. But it's amazing to me how often and how readily people choose to ignore the truth about what it takes to achieve their goals.

Let's say, for example, that you want to go to law school. Certainly your hope is to become a lawyer, or at least earn your law degree. That's a goal that seems clear enough. And it's a goal that anyone with average intelligence and sufficient drive and discipline can achieve.

Let's say you are an intelligent, driven, disciplined *working mother* who wants to go to law school. That changes things a bit, doesn't it? It's no longer just you and the challenge of completing law school. Now it's you -- *and* your husband *and* the kids *and* dinner *and* daycare *and* school plays *and* Little League *and* the measles *and* shopping *and* housekeeping*and* the entire PTA -- *and* the challenge of completing law school.

Your goal is still achievable (the list of obstacles above isn't that different from the list I faced myself several years ago when I decided to go back to school for my MBA). But in this situation it's not simply a matter of picking up your acceptance letter, buying your books and heading for the classroom. It's clearly going to take lots of sacrifices from both you *and* your family.

Let's say these facts are so intimidating that you just can't face them. You look at your goal and the obstacles you will have to overcome and you say to yourself, "Naw, it won't be that bad. Four hours a week of night school for a few months and I'm there, baby. This won't interfere with my family life or my job much."

This kind of self delusion is so destructive it will undermine your goals more quickly than any obstacle you care to name. When you lie to yourself in this way, you fail to see your goal clearly; and you fail to see what it's going to take to achieve that goal. You fail to gauge the time involved, the effort required and the obstacles to be overcome. Inevitably, you will fail to plan for those things and to enlist the kind of family help and support you will need to accomplish your goal.

And though you've chosen not to recognize the problems that lie ahead, I guarantee they will wait for you.

Talk To Your Teammates

If we are going to get people to help us achieve our ends, we must be able to communicate our goals clearly. That's your *message*. It's not enough to see our goals ourselves, our followers must see them, too. And they must see *exactly* what kind of help or support we need to achieve those goals.

Because our lives today are filled with so many, not merely competing goals, but *conflicting priorities*, this is tougher than it sounds.

EXAMPLE. Having come to grips with the facts of her situation, Working Mom is still determined to go to law school. But now she knows she will have to enlist the aid of her family in her quest for a JD. Her husband will have to help more with the kids, feeding them, driving them to school and soccer practice. Both her husband and her kids will have to help more around the house with the cooking and cleaning. And everyone will have to leave her alone so she can study.

In other words, she will not really be able to look after her family for about two years. If she decides to sugarcoat the situation, this message will be distorted, and she will lose her credibility when the truth comes out. She will confuse her family ("If this is supposed to be easy, there must be something wrong with me") and she'll create resentment -- even resistance -- to her goals. And Working Mom will, in the end, rob her family of the good feelings they could have had about themselves for helping out.

Who's On First?

All this is not to say that in communicating our messages about our goals we have to overwhelm our potential followers with all the horrible details. In fact, it's a good idea to break our messages down into bite-sized pieces.

But sometimes all our efforts to do this just don't work. Why? Chances are we've failed to focus on the needs of our followers. Human beings, remember, tend to look at things from a what's-in-it-for-me point of view and we've got to keep that in mind or we'll have a heck of a time enlisting their support for our plan.

Now don't get me wrong: I've seen more examples of human unselfishness and generosity in my life than I could possibly fit into a single book. But I've also found that it's a reality of human nature that, when deciding whether to support a particular leader's goals, we tend to focus on how that support will fulfill our own needs.

So, even if you're as effective a communicator as Ronald Reagan, if you don't communicate in terms of the benefits to your potential followers, who's going to listen?

To illustrate this point, let's go back to our Working Mom. She makes the following announcement at dinner one night:

"Okay everybody, listen up! I've decided to go back to school. It's going to be tough, but I'm determined, and you'll all have to do your part. Bob, you'll have to forget about the company softball team; you'll be too busy running the kids around to soccer practice and Brownie meetings.

And Junior, you'll have to learn to dress yourself and make your own bed. Suzy, you'll have to start helping with the cooking. And all of you will have to give me *lots* of space. I'll have studying to do every night. All this means a lot to me and my feelings of fulfillment as a human being. Well, whaddaya think? Can I count on your support?"

Not bloody likely! (I wouldn't even support her after a speech like that.)

But what if our Working Mom said something like this: "It means a lot to me that you are all willing to give me the freedom I need to do what I need to do. Now, what can I do to make all of this easier for you?"

Bingo! Oh, she may get some grousing at first, but in the end she'll know what her followers need. She'll know who's playing what base and she'll be able to give them (just as Dale's manager did) what they need to get the job done.

Then, of course, she must focus on one of her followers' most important needs: the *need for recognition*.

"Bob, you've been really great about this. I think this will make our relationship much stronger. Junior, you sure are a big boy to help out like this! And Suzy! Wow! I knew I could count on your help, but you've been terrific! In fact, without all of your support, I just wouldn't be able to do this at all. Thanks, guys!"

The difference is, in the second example, Working Mom focused on how her potential followers will benefit by supporting her goals and how they needed to feel to be willing to do it.

Along with your follower's feelings, you will need to focus on and assess three other important characteristics of your followers:

Ability. Ask yourself this question: Can they do it? Do your potential followers actually have the skills and the knowledge they need to do what you want them to do to support you in your efforts?

Willingness. Are your followers motivated to do the job? Have you compensated them enough, either with salary, praise or recognition? Is your remuneration enough to enlist their support? In other words, do they want what you're offering enough to want to see you succeed?

Maturity. Can your followers direct their own behavior? When you consider their abilities and their willingness, do they describe someone who has the understanding, the skills and the motivation to undertake the task you have in mind and see it through *on their own?*

Remember: Maturity only bears a superficial relationship to age. In our culture we keep people immature and dependent much longer than other cultures. Just because someone is 30 years old doesn't mean he's mature.

THE ESSENCE OF LEADERSHIP

The American workforce is changing. As we move into the next century, fewer young people and more women and elderly are entering or remaining in the job market. And as the Baby Boom generation ages, observers expect a veritable traffic jam of middle-aged middle managers honking and yelling half-way down the corporate highway.

It's not just workforce demographics that are changing; workers' *expectations* are changing as well. And their growing concerns about family, lifestyle and quality of life are creating new challenges for community and business leaders in the 90s.

Challenges, yes, but also, opportunities. Among other things, all this change is going to produce a tremendous demand for competent, effective leadership.

And you, Kemosabi, are on the road to becoming just that: an effective leader. But I believe that leadership is not something you can absorb exclusively from the pages of a book. More than nearly any concept I have tried to communicate here, leadership requires hands-on learning.

The best place to start is with yourself. If you apply all of the preceding principles to your own life, you will create a *self-management system*. And self management is the essence of leadership.

Ask yourself: What are my abilities? What do I know? What do I need to find out? What are my goals? What do I need to do to achieve these goals? What do I need -- time, skills, money -- to do the job right? What am I willing to do -- not what my mother expects me to do -- but on what am I really *willing* to spend my time and energy? How do I need to feel about these goals to care enough to spend my time and energy on them?

By taking yourself in hand, by asking yourself these hard questions and answering them honestly, you will be taking the first and most important step toward becoming an effective leader.

THE ACID TEST

Your efforts to influence people in your community are the ultimate "acid test" of your leadership skills. If you can handle yourself in this arena, you can handle your personal and business leadership challenges with one power base tied behind your back. I see lots of people who, for various reasons, are ineffective personally and in business but who absolutely *bloom* in community leadership roles. Then I watch them take their new found leadership skills back to their jobs, to their personal challenges, where they find that their effectiveness has improved a hundred-fold.

You see, in a community leadership situation, you have a chance to experiment, to make mistakes, get beaten to a pulp once in awhile, and learn -- *without* too many serious consequences. Certainly you don't want to fall on your face every time you take on a Jaycee project or try to raise funds for the United Way. But if you do, the consequences are much less serious than such failures would be on the job or even at home.

You get a different kind of feedback from your community than you do in your work environment or at home. When you're out there, working with people who don't love you and are not "buying" you, their reactions to you and your work and leadership style are much more raw and unguarded -- a lot more *real*.

I can name hundreds of examples of people who have gone out to work in their communities and found the world opening up for them, with every ounce of their community altruism paying off in personal benefits, in business contacts and in friendships they would never have made any other way. But one man in particular stands out in my experience as a person who gained more from his community leadership than he ever put into it -- and he put in a lot.

EXAMPLE. Joe was a local bank manager for over 25 years. In that time, he did business with a huge number of people in his community. But the reason those people remember him has nothing to do with his job.

"When I think about Joe," one of his bank customers told me one day, "I guess I never think of him in his banker's suit. I always see him in red Long-Johns and a long, white beard, ringing his bell outside the post office."

Year after year at Christmas time, Joe stood out on the post office steps, ringing his bell for the Kiwanis Club and the Salvation Army. In the two decades he worked his kettle, the Kiwanis raised more money to fight blindness and help handicapped kids than ever in the history of the organization.

"Well, what I remember," Joe says of his years of community service, "is all the fun I've had. It wasn't really a sacrifice at all. I loved to do it."

There was never any confusion in Joe's mind about what he was doing. Sure, he got a lot of business from his community involvement, but that was never his *goal*. He put his name and his credibility on the line for this particular community service project and his genuine joy was so evident that passersby wanted to stand beside him and ring, too.

That's leadership!

JUST DO IT!

By reading through this book, you've increased your awareness of your own potential growth in the realm of personal effectiveness. You have offered yourself the gift of growth and informed choices.

Ask yourself, "What am I going to do *right now* to start creating my behavior, to make my relationships more productive and satisfying or to get a grip on my time and stress levels?

Actions are what count -- not only with others, but on your own internal yardstick. By taking just *one* suggestion, by implementing just *one* needed change or by making just *one* positive choice -- you can be assured you are on your way. You'll know it, and so will those who discuss you when you leave the room. I know. A fly told me so.

INDEX

207

ACKNOWLEDGEMENTS

The monolithic undertaking of conceiving, researching and producing a book would not be possible without the tremendous effort and support of many dedicated people. I would like to publicly acknowledge these contributions.

John Waters, for professional writing and awesome personal support.

Mary McGrath, for the book's design, accuracy and production.

Paula Munier Lee, an excellent editor and helpful collaborator.

Anita Cullinan, AMC Indexing, for a timely and professional indexing job.

Jerry Takigawa, Takigawa Design, for the brilliant cover design.

Grant Hamilton, for being the photographer of my dreams.

Susan Joyce, for an excellent proofreading job.

Chuck Revill, Community Press, for unlimited advice and excellent production.

Rita Coronel, R. Goldberg & Associates, whose unselfish advice and help got me "unstuck."

And my numerous friends, clients and loving family members whose comments and suggestions have shaped the work.

ACKNOWLEDGEMENTS

The monolithic undertaking of conceiving, researching and producing a book would not be possible without the tremendous effort and support of many dedicated people. I would like to publicly acknowledge these contributions.

John Waters, for professional writing and awesome personal support.
Mary McGrath, for the book's design, accuracy and production.
Mike Miller, for the successful role model of personal effectiveness that she is.
Paula Munier Lee, an excellent editor and helpful collaborator.
Anita Cullinan, AMC Indexing, for a timely and professional indexing job.
Patricia Rain and Susan Joyce, for excellent proofreading services.
Chuck Revill, Community Press, for unlimited advice and excellent production.
Wendy Brickman, Brickman Marketing for energetic, innovative, action oriented marketing support.
Rita Coronel, R. Goldberg & Associates, whose unselfish advice and help got me "unstuck."
And my numerous friends, clients and loving family members whose comments and suggestions have shaped the work.

ABOUT THE AUTHOR

Brigid McGrath Massie is a business consultant, counselor and professional speaker who operates her own consulting and training firm. For more than a decade she has designed and delivered customized supervisory, managerial and sales training programs to large and small companies throughout the United States and Europe. Her list of clients includes Pacific Bell, Vintner's International and McCormick & Company, among others.

A popular keynote speaker, Brigid imparts to her audiences both the practical tools *and* the motivation to be their best.

Brigid holds two Master's degrees. Her Master's in Business Administration is from Pepperdine University, and she earned a Master's degree in Social Work from California State University in Fresno, California.

Recognized as "One of the Five Women In Northern California Who Make A Difference," Brigid's work has also received national attention through the Athena Award for *Business Woman Of the Year*.

Brigid is currently working on her second book, tentatively titled: *Selling: Not the World's Oldest Profession. A Guidebook for Selling Success for the Non-Salesperson.*

Brigid resides in Salinas, California with her husband, Dan, and children, Andrea and Kevin, and the family Sheltie, "Indiana Jones."

ABOUT THE WRITER

John Kevin Waters is a freelance writer/editor living and working in the Bay Area of California.

Over the years he has contributed a wide variety of news, features, columns and reviews to such publications as: *San Jose Magazine, Monterey Life, The Silicon Valley Insider* and *The Salinas Californian,* among others.

Mr. Waters has co-authored two other books: *The Salinas Valley: An Illustrated History,* which he wrote with Denzel and Jenny Verardo; and *Silicon Valley: Inventing the Future,* which he wrote with Jean Deitz Sexton.

Waters is a graduate of the University of I⟨ and currently resides in Los Altos, California with wife, Gina.

Bibliography and Recommended Reading List

Adams, J. L. *Conceptual Blockbusting.* 2nd Ed. New York: W. W. Norton and Company, 1979.

Beck, Arthur C. and Hillmar, Ellis D. *Positive Management Practices.* San Francisco: Jossey-Bass Publishers, 1986.

Bensen, Herbert, and Klipper, Miriam Z. *The Relaxation Response.* New York: Avon, 1976.

Blanchard, Kenneth, and Peale, Norman Vincent. *The Power of Ethical Management.* New York: Morrow, 1988.

Bolles, Richard N. *What Color is Your Parachute?* Updated ed. Berkeley: Ten Speed Press, 1987.

Brod, Craig and St. John, Wes. *Technostress: The Human Cost of the Computer Revolution.* Toronto: Addison-Wesley, 1983.

Burley-Allen, Madeline. *Listening: The Forgotten Skill.* New York: John Wiley and Sons, 1982.

Campbell, Jeremy. *Winston Churchill's Afternoon Nap: A Wide-Awake Inquiry into the Human Nature of Time.* New York: Simon & Schuster, 1987.

Connellan, Thomas K. *How to Grow People Into Self-Starters.* Ann Arbor: The Achievement Institute, 1980.

Cooper, Cary L. *Improving Interpersonal Relations: A Guide To Social Skill Development for Managers and Group Leaders.* New Jersey: Prentice-Hall, 1982.

Cousins, Norman. *Anatomy of an Illness As Perceived by the Patient.* New York: Bantam, 1981.

Cousins, Norman. *The Healing Heart.* New York: Avon, 1984.

Crawford, R. *The Techniques of Creative Thinking.* New York: Holt, Rinehart, & Winston, 1971.

DeBono, Edward. *Lateral Thinking.* New York: Harper & Row, 1990.

DeBono, Edward. *The Use of Lateral Thinking.* New York: Penguin, 1990.

Dienhart, Ligita, and Pinsel, E. Melvin. *Power Lunching.* Chicago: Turnbull and Willoughby, 1985.

Doyle, M. and Straus, D. *How To Make Meetings Work.* New York: Playboy Paperbacks, 1976.

Drucker, Peter F. *The Changing World of the Executive.* New York: Times Books, 1982.

Drucker, Peter F. *Managing for Results*. New York: Harper & Row, 1964.

Dunsing, Richard J. *You and I Have Simply Got To Stop Meeting This Way*. New York: Amacom, 1978.

Ford, Betty, and Chase, Chris. *Betty: A Glad Awakening*. New York: Doubleday, 1987.

Garfield, Charles. *Peak Performers: The New Heroes of American Business*. New York: Avon, 1987.

Gordon, Thomas. *Leader Effectiveness Training*. New York: Bantam Books, 1977.

Grodon, William J. J. *Synectics*. New York: Harper & Row, 1961.

Grothe, Marcey and Wylie, Peter. *Problem Bosses: Who They Are and How To Deal with Them*. New York: Fawcett, 1988.

Hanson, Peter G. M.D., *Stress for Success*. New York: Ballantine Books, 1989.

Harvey-Jones, John. *Make It Happen: Reflections on Leadership*. London: William Collins and Sons.

Helmstedder, Shad. *The Self-Talk Solution*. New York: Pocket Books, 1987.

Hersey, Paul and Kenneth H. Blanchard. *Management of Organizational Behavior: Utilizing Human Resources*. 2nd Ed. New Jersey: Prentice-Hall, 1972.

Hochheiser, Robert M. *How to Work for a Jerk: Your Success Is the Best Revenge*. New York: Vintage, 1987.

Johnson, Spencer, M.D. *One Minute for Myself*. New York: Avon Books, 1985.

Kepner, C. H. and B. B. Tregoe. *The Rational Manager*. New York: McGraw-Hill, 1965.

King, Patricia. *Never Work for a Jerk!* Danbury: Watts, 1987.

Leider, Richard J. *The Power of Purpose*. New York: Ballantine Books, 1985.

Levering, Robert; Mosokowitz, Milton, and Katz, Michael. *The 100 Best Companies to Work for in America*. New York: Signet, 1987.

Likert, Rensis and Jane Gibson Likert. *New Ways of Managing Conflict*. New York: McGraw-Hill, 1976.

Mackay, Harvey. *Swim With the Sharks, Without Being Eaten Alive*. New York: Morrow, 1988.

Meyers, Gerald C., and Holusha, John. *When It Hits The Fan: Managing The Nine Crises of Business.* Boston: Houghton Mifflin, 1986.

Naisbitt, John. *Megatrends: Ten New Directions Transforming Our Lives.* 6th Ed. New York: Warner, 1983.

Naisbitt, John, and Aburdene, Patricia. *Reinventing the Corporation: Transforming Your Job and Your Company for the New Information Society.* New York: Warner, 1985.

Onken, William Jr. *Managing Management Time: Who's Got the Monkey?* Englewood Cliffs: Prentice-Hall, 1984.

Peck, M. Scott. *The Road Less Traveled.* New York: Touchstone, 1980.

Peters, Thomas, and Austin, Nancy. *A Passion for Excellence: The Leadership Difference.* New York: Random House, 1985.

Peters, Tom. *Thriving on Chaos: A Revolutionary Agenda for Today's Manager.* New York: Knopf, 1987.

Plunkett, Lorne C. and Guy A Hale. *The Proactive Manager.* New York: John Wiley & Sons, 1982.

Roskies, Ethel. *Stress Management for the Healthy Type A: Theory and Practice.* Guilford Press, 1987.

Shaevitz, Marjorie Helen. *The Superwoman Syndrome.* New York: Warner, 1985.

Taylor, Harold L. *Making Time Work for You: A Guidebook to Effective and Productive Time Management.* New York: Beaufort, 1982.

Waitley, Dennis. *The Psychology of Winning.* New York: Berkley, 1984.

Waterman Jr., Robert H. *The Renewal Factor: How the Best Get and Keep the Competitive Edge.* New York: Bantam, 1987.

Watson, Thomas J. *A Business and Its Beliefs: The Ideas That Helped Build IBM.* New York: McGraw-Hill, 1963.

Wells, Joel. *Coping in the Eighties: Eliminating Needless Stress and Guilt.* Thomas More, 1986.

Ziglar, Zig. *Top Performance: How to Develop Excellence in Yourself and Others.* New York: Berkley, 1987.

INDEX

What Do They Say When You Leave the Room?

How to Increase Your Personal Effectiveness
At Home, At Work, and In Your Life

Order Form

To order more copies of *What Do They Say When You Leave The Room?*, complete the form below and mail it to:

> Eudemonia Publications
> P. O. Box 373
> Salinas, CA. 93902
>
> For telephone orders:
> 1-800-244-6488 or (408) 757-8514

Name ————————————————————

Address ———————————————————

City/State/Zip ————————————————

# of books ordered: ——— $10.95 per book ———

California Tax, 7.75% (.85)   ———
Only if ordering in California
Postage/handling $ 1.50 per book   ———
$1.50 1st one, $.50 each additional

Total due:

Make check or money order payable to Eudemonia Publications.

For Visa or Mastercard   Card #_____

Expiration Date _____   Signature _____
Thank You!